# UNDERSTANDING U.S. AND GLOBAL ECONOMIC TRENDS

## A Guide for the Non-Economist

### Second Edition

Daniel Gaske

**KENDALL/HUNT PUBLISHING COMPANY**
4050 Westmark Drive     Dubuque, Iowa 52002

Printed in the United States of America
10  9  8  7  6  5  4  3  2  1

Dedicated to Susan, Anne, Dave, and Kelley.

# | Contents

# | Preface

After almost 25 years of practicing and teaching economics, I have come to believe that for many people interested in understanding today's economic trends, a book is needed that has a different approach from many standard textbooks. This is an attempt to provide such a book.

The book takes as its audience people who do not need to become economists, but who simply need or want a better basic understanding of the economic system in which they live. It is in particular written for the individual who wants on his or her own to obtain a self-taught better understanding of economics, to be used much as one would use a computer users guide to understand better the operation of a computer. At the same time, the book could be utilized in economics survey classes.

The book focuses on areas of economics that are most prominent in newspapers and magazines — such as growth, inflation, unemployment, interest rates, the budget deficit, the Federal Reserve, the trade balance, the exchange rate, and competitiveness. It begins by laying out how economists measure the economic trends of nations (Chapters 1 and 2). It then discusses basic principles of economics such as supply, demand, price, and how markets function (Chapter 3), and uses these principles to build simple frameworks for understanding nations' domestic and international economic performances (Chapters 4-6).

The book then turns to how fiscal and monetary policies work (Chapters 7 and 8) and continues by discussing patterns of international trade and how government policy impacts on those patterns (Chapters 9 and 10). The book concludes by examining factors that determine the long-run economic success or failure of nations (Chapter 11) and how the world economic system is changing (Chapter 12).

Each chapter makes extensive use of real world economic trends, including the 1997-98 financial crises in East Asia and Russia, to illustrate how the principles laid out have performed in the US and global economy, and avoids as much as possible the use of graphs and equations as explanatory devices. Each chapter also concludes with a concise summary of the key concepts presented and discussed in the chapter, and the book contains an index to key terms and concepts.

A final feature of the book is that each chapter focuses very tightly on a particular economic topic. As a result, it is very easy for a reader, or instructor, to go through the material in a different manner than laid out in the book. For example, if a reader desired to examine fiscal and monetary policy before looking at causes of international balance of payments and exchange rate trends, he or she could simply jump from Chapter 5 to Chapters 7 and 8 before returning to Chapter 6.

# 1 | Measuring Nations' Domestic Economic Performances

While many economics books begin with discussion of basic economic concepts, with which most people are unfamiliar, this book starts with actual measures used to describe economic trends in the United States and other nations — concepts such as unemployment, inflation, recession and trade balances — that generally are more familiar. This chapter discusses the measures used to assess the domestic economic performance of a nation, and the next chapter examines measures of a nation's international economic situation.

These measures, which we often see on the front pages of newspapers, are important in many ways. They guide the decisions of business, consumers, and government decisionmakers and provide basic data for automatic adjustment of certain economic variables, such as the use that is made of consumer price inflation to adjust payments to social security recipients. These measures also often have political impact by affecting how citizens vote in elections, as occurred in the Presidential election of 1996 when economic expansion and low inflation likely played an important role in the re-election of President Clinton.

While literally thousands of these measures are available in total, four stand out in the assessment of nations' domestic economic performance. It is these measures — changes in real GDP, inflation rate, unemployment rate, and interest rates — on which this chapter focuses.

## Real Gross Domestic or National Product (GDP/GNP) and Its Rate of Change

Probably the single most widely used measure of a country's domestic economic performance is gross domestic or national product (GDP or GNP) and the rate at which its real component changes. GDP and GNP, while slightly different in the specifics of their definitions (see Figure 1-1), each measure essentially the same thing, the total value of production that occurs in a nation's economy for final consumption within some time period, usually a year or a quarter of a year — January-March, October-

December, etc. However, in terms of assessing an economy's performance, it is not the level of GDP that is most important, but the rate of change in the real component — real GDP — since the latter allows a judgment to be made as whether the overall level of actual output or production in the economy is rising or falling and hence whether the economy is becoming better off or worse off.

The computation of GDP is carried out by nations' central statistical agencies — in the case of the United States by the Bureau of Economic Analysis of the Department of Commerce — and is first computed in what is called nominal terms. By nominal terms, economists mean that valuation of the output of an economy has been done at prices that prevailed in each particular time period. In other words, nominal GDP contains changes in the value of production due partially to inflation.

To use this definition of GDP that includes inflation to assess whether or how fast actual production is rising would be badly flawed. A high inflation rate, for example, could cause nominal GDP to rise even when the actual level of production — real GDP — was falling. Because of this potential distortion, economists carry out a process called deflating. In effect, using statistical techniques, the inflation component is eliminated from nominal GDP to produce real GDP.

### Figure 1-1 Differences between GDP and GNP

Economists define the total value of production of a nation according to two similar definitions — gross domestic product, or GDP, and gross national product, or GNP. GDP measures the value of production on a geographic basis. That is, it includes in a nation's GDP all the value added to production within the country's geographic boundaries, regardless of who owns the economic resources that provided the production. Thus, in the case of the United States, the value of production attributed to the investments made by Japanese automobile companies in their US plants is included in US GDP, but not in US GNP. In contrast, GNP is a ownership based definition. It includes in a nation's GNP the value of production produced by its firms, even if they are located abroad. In the case of the United States, GNP includes the value of production added, in effect the profits, by US companies' factories abroad.

In most cases, the value of GNP and GDP are quite close together; this is the case for the United States. In 1997, for example, US GDP was $8.08 trillion and US GNP was $8.06 trillion, a difference of less than 0.2 percent. Only when a country has a large amount of either outward or inward foreign investment relative to the total size of its economy will GNP and GDP significantly differ. The United States now uses GDP as the primary way in which it releases its national production and income statistics, after changing from using GNP in the late 1980s.

Once real GDP is arrived at, it is then used as the basis for judgments about countries' economic performance.

- When real GDP is falling, the economy is said to be in recession; if the fall is extremely large, the economy is said to be in depression.

- When real GDP is rising at what is thought to be a creditable rate, the economy is said to be in expansion.

- When real GDP is rising, but barely, the term stagnation often is used to describe the country's economic performance.

- When real GDP is rising very rapidly, the economy generally is said to be in an economic boom or overheated. Obviously, what is desired is an economic expansion — i.e., rapid real growth but not so rapid as to be unsustainable.

Over time, most economies experience all of these growth situations. In the United States, for example: real GDP expanded over 6 percent in 1984 in a particularly rapid expansion — maybe an economic boom; barely expanded at all in the stagnation year of 1992; and declined in the recession years of 1974-75, 1980, 1982, and 1991 (see Figure 1-2). Once in this century, US real GDP plunged, falling by over one third between 1930 and 1933 in what we call the Great Depression. These variations in growth are often referred to as the business cycle.

On average, US real GDP increased about 3 percent a year over the last 40 years, while other countries have had different experiences with real GDP growth (see Figure 1-3).

## Rate of Inflation

Another important measure of an economy's performance is its inflation rate — i.e., how fast the overall price level is increasing. An economy's inflation rate also is compiled by some component of its central statistical agency; in the case of the United States it is the Bureau of Labor Statistics.

To obtain the inflation rate, these agencies first carry out surveys of prices in the economy and, using statistical techniques, create an index of the important prices, with each price counting in proportion to the amount of spending on that item. In the consumer price index, for example, housing costs receive a large weight in the index, while prices of restaurant food receive a much smaller weight, since the typical consumer spends a lot on the former and only a small amount on the latter.

Figure 1-2  US Real GDP Growth

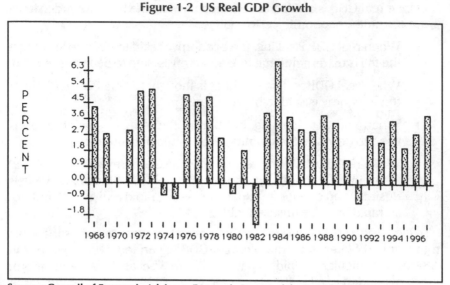

Source: Council of Economic Advisers, *Economic Report of the President, 1998.*

Figure 1-3  US and Foreign Real GDP Growth, 1985-95 (percent per year)

| | |
|---|---|
| United States | 2.4 |
| Japan | 2.8 |
| Germany | 2.6 |
| France | 2.2 |
| South Korea | 8.9 |
| Mexico | 0.9 |
| India | 5.2 |
| China | 9.8 |

Source: Central Intelligence Agency, *Handbook of International Economic Statistics, 1996*

The final step in computing the inflation rate is identical to the final step in computing changes in real GDP — calculating the percentage change in the price index over some period, such as a year, quarter, or month. Frequently, as is also often the case for changes in real GDP, percentage changes calculated for less than a year are expressed as "at an annual rate", which is the rate that would occur if the monthly or quarterly changes continued for a full year. These annual rates will be roughly 4 times the actual change for a quarterly change and 12 times the actual change for a monthly change, but will not be exactly 4 or 12 times because of the impact of compounding, an effect similar to that which occurs when your bank gives you "an interest rate of 6 percent compounded daily for an annual yield of 6.5 percent."

For a number of reasons, economists regard a lower inflation rate as better than a higher one.

- Higher inflation tends to disrupt the economic decision process, since it makes it difficult to know how to evaluate future values of prices and incomes. For example, a promise by your employer to raise your wages 5 percent a year for the next four years may or may not be a good promise for you, depending on the rate of inflation. If inflation over this period is 2 percent a year, the promise will have been a good one, since your real earnings would have risen 3 percent a year. If, on the other hand, inflation is 9 percent a year, the outcome for you would not be particularly favorable, since your real income would have declined 4 percent a year.

- Higher inflation causes losses in real incomes for people who have fixed money incomes. Since pensioners are often in this group, public policy tends to be concerned about these re-distributional aspects of inflation.

- Higher inflation often pushes individuals into higher tax brackets and raises their tax payments even though the increased incomes may be strictly due to higher inflation with real incomes having not risen at all.

- In today's integrated world economic system, higher inflation in one country will mean that country's prices will be rising relative to prices in other countries, and the higher prices in the first country will steadily reduce its international trade competitiveness and lead to undesirable impacts on jobs, incomes, and the country's international economic trends.

- Finally, inflation sometimes gets really out of control and moves into a situation known as hyperinflation. In this situation, inflation is measured not in percent, or tens of percent, or hundreds of percent, but in thousands of percent a year. For example, the hyperinflation rate in Bolivia in the mid-1980s was 12,000 percent a year. Once inflation gets into this range, the money of the country becomes near-worthless and the real economy of the country soon grinds to a halt as people refuse to accept ever-more worthless money as payment. This last process has been part of Russia's economic woes in the 1990s.

Like real GDP growth, countries' inflation rates have tended to vary widely over time. In the United States, the amount of this variation has been relatively mild, as has average inflation. The highest yearly US inflation rate since the end of World War II has been 14 percent in 1974 and the lowest rate 1 percent a year during the 1950s (see Figure 1-4). Other countries, such as Brazil, have experienced much more variation in inflation rates (see Figure 1-5).

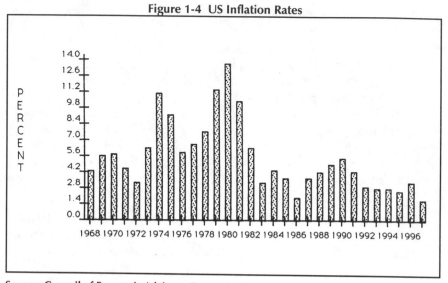

Figure 1-4  US Inflation Rates

Source: Council of Economic Advisers, *Economic Report of the President, 1998.*

Figure 1-5  US and Foreign Peak Inflation Rates, 1960s to 1990s (percent)

| | |
|---|---|
| United States | 14 (1980) |
| Germany | 7 (1974) |
| France | 14 (1974) |
| Mexico | 132 (1987) |
| Brazil | 2669 (1994) |
| Israel | 374 (1984) |
| Turkey | 110 (1980) |

Source: International Monetary Fund, *International Financial Statistics, Yearbook 1995.*

## Unemployment Rate

The measure of domestic economic performance with which most people are perhaps most familiar is the unemployment rate. This rate is a measure of the extent to which there are people unsuccessfully looking for jobs. It too is calculated by a government statistical agency; for the United States, it is carried out by the Bureau of Labor Statistics and the Census Bureau.

To better understand the unemployment rate, it is useful to begin with the categories into which the population is divided in terms of labor market situation. First, the population is allocated between those individuals either working or seeking work, called the "labor force", and those individuals neither working nor seeking work. This latter group is called "not in the labor force" and is made up of a wide variety of individuals —

children, retired persons, fulltime students, parents who do not work, etc. In the United States, about 137 million people are in the labor force and about 130 million are not.

The next step in determining the unemployment rate is to take the number of persons in the labor force and divide it between the number of persons employed and the number who, while actively seeking employment, have been unable to find it — i.e. the unemployed. For the United States, this step produced, in 1997, 130 million employed and 7 million unemployed. The unemployment rate itself, 4.9 percent for 1997, is obtained by dividing the number of unemployed by the labor force.

In what should be no surprise, unemployment and the unemployment rate also varies over the business cycle. The 20th Century peak in the United States was reached during the Great Depression, when the unemployment rate exceeded 25 percent. Since World War II, the highest yearly rate has been 9.7 percent in 1982 and the lowest rate 2.9 percent in 1953 (see Figure 1-6).

Figure 1-6 US Unemployment Rates

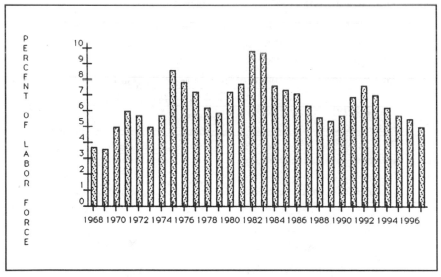

Source: Council of Economic Advisers, *Economic Report of the President, 1998*.

Unlike inflation rates and changes in real GDP, where international comparisons can be made fairly directly, the differences that exist across countries in how unemployment rates are defined, obtained, and calculated make difficult such comparisons of unemployment rates and should be made with care. That said, it is nonetheless useful to put the present US unemployment situation in international context with the observation that, on various countries' own definitions, US unemployment is substantially lower than that of Europe and about the same as that of Japan.

## Interest Rates

A final measure by which domestic economic performance of a country is judged is the level of interest rates — i.e., the price paid to borrow money. For instance, a mortgage interest rate of 7 percent means that if an individual borrows a certain amount of money to build a house, each year 7 percent of the amount of the loan not paid back must be paid to the lender in interest. So, in effect, the price paid by borrowers, or received by lenders, for the use of this money is the interest rate.

In a complex economy like the United States, there are many interest rates, each of which connect to a particular kind of borrowing or lending (see Figure 1-7).

- The widely-cited prime rate is the rate that major banks charge the most credit-worthy borrowers on short-term, unsecured loans.

- Mortgage rates are the rates that individuals and businesses pay when they borrow money for long periods of time and secure that money with a mortgage on real property like a house, commercial building, or land.

- The discount rate is an interest rate that the US central bank, the Federal Reserve System (see Chapter 8), charges on money it loans to commercial banks.

- Bond yields are implicit interest rates that governments or corporations pay on bonds they sell to raise money. For example, if you buy a $100 US Savings Bond that matures in five years, you will pay less than $100 for the bond. The difference between what you pay and the $100 that you receive when the bond matures is the implicit interest rate on that bond.

**Figure 1-7  US Interest Rates: Types and Levels, 1997 (percent)**

| Prime Rate | 8.4 | Federal Funds Rate | 5.5 |
|---|---|---|---|
| Discount Rate | 5.0 | Mortgage Rates | 7.7 |
| AAA Corporate Bonds | 7.3 | Municipal Bonds | 5.6 |
| US 3-Month Securities | 5.1 | US 10-Year Bonds | 6.3 |

Source: Council of Economic Advisers, *Economic Report of the President, 1998.*

While there are many types of interest rates, using them as a performance measure for the domestic economy is made easier by the fact that for the most part interest rates tend to move up and down together, although not in lock step. In general, long-term interest rates, like bond yields and mortgage rates, fluctuate less than do short-term interest rates, like the prime rate. For example, in the United States, in 1982, a period of high interest rates, the prime rate rose for a time to in excess of 20 percent while mortgage rates rose to 15 percent. In early 1994, a period of relative

### Figure 1-8  Trends in US Interest Rates

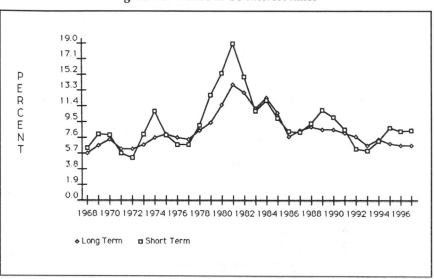

Source: Council of Economic Advisers, *Economic Report of the President, 1998.*

low interest rates, the prime rate fell all the way to 3 percent, but mortgage rates came down only to 6-7 percent (see Figure 1-8).

A final aspect of interest rates is the concept of the real interest rate. The real interest rate is an attempt to account for the impact of inflation on interest rates and on economic decisions. For example, to borrow money at 7 percent to buy a house or build a factory when prices of housing or the output the factory could produce are rising at 20 percent is very different than borrowing money at 7 percent to do those activities when prices are stable — i.e., there is no inflation at all. Specifically, borrowing the money is a much better decision in the first situation than the second since the higher inflation will mean the value of what is being bought or produced with the borrowed money is rising faster than the cost of borrowing the money.

The real interest rate concept addresses this issue by defining the real interest rate as the nominal interest rate — i.e. the rate of interest actually quoted and set into a borrowing/lending contract — minus the rate of inflation. This procedure accounts for distortions on borrowing and lending decisions of inflation and is thought by economists to be a better way to view interest rates. In the example given in the previous paragraph, for example, interest rates as measured by the real interest rate in the first case were not only low but a -13 percent (7-20), while real interest rates in the second case were a relatively high 7 percent (7-0).

Real interest rates also have shown considerable fluctuation over time in the United States. In the late 1970s, for example, even with nominal interest rates high, real interest rates were low because of high inflation rates; not surprisingly, borrowing levels were high despite the high nominal rates, in response to the low, and occasionally negative, real interest rates. In contrast, 1993's low nominal long-term interest rates were in real terms not all that low because of the low inflation rate of that year. You can verify these observations by subtracting the inflation rates in Figure 1-4 from the interest rates in Figure 1-8.

For the most part, economists regard lower interest rates, especially real interest rates, as preferable. Low interest rates provide benefits by making it less expensive for consumers to borrow and spend and for businesses to borrow, invest and expand capacity. However, if real interest rates become negative, economists become concerned, since negative returns will cause lenders to stop lending and/or move their money out of the country.

## Summary

1. Four measures describe the main domestic economic trends in a country — changes in real GDP, inflation rate, unemployment rate, and interest rates.

2. Changes in real GDP show whether and how fast the overall level of production in the economy is growing; positive changes are better.

3. The inflation rate shows how fast the overall level of prices in the economy — often measured by the consumer price index — is rising; lower is better.

4. The unemployment rate shows the extent of joblessness in the economy; lower is better.

5. Interest rates, of which there are many different ones, show how much it costs to borrow money in the economy; lower is better, especially with regard to the so-called real rate of interest, so long as the rate stays positive.

# 2 | Measuring Nations' International Economic Situations

Ten years ago, measures of a nation's international economic situation would not have been included as one of the key measures of US economic performance. Even today, many books relegate it to near the end of the book. However, with the increased integration of the US economy into the world economy — illustrated by the impacts in 1998 of the Asian and Russian financial problems on the US stock market — it is necessary to include measures of a country's international economic performance early on in an assessment of its overall economic situation.

In assessing nations' international economic situations, economists make use of two main measures. One is the international balance of payments, made up of a number of sub-components, such as the trade and current account. The other is the exchange rates for a nation's currency in terms of other currencies and changes in those exchange rates.

## The International Balance of Payments

The international balance of payments is a system of accounts that records flows of funds (money) into and out of a country to and from the rest of world. These flows of funds occur for a variety of reasons — to make purchases, to make gifts, to invest — and the balance of payments of accounts are structured around these activities.

### Credits, Debits, Surpluses, and Deficits

Before getting into the components of the balance of payments accounts, however, it will be useful to first lay out the concepts of credits, debits, surpluses, and deficits. To begin, a balance of payments transaction for a country occurs when there is a flow of funds across a country's border. When this flow goes out of the country, for example as a payment for imported goods, it is recorded as a balance of payments debit, or negative item. When the flow of funds is into the country, for example, to make an investment in the country, it is recorded as a credit, or positive item.

When credit flows exceed debit flows in the balance of payments, a surplus is said to be occurring. When the debit flows exceed the credit flows, a deficit is said to be occurring. So, for the United States, the trade deficit that is prominent in the news means that, for trade purposes, more money is being spent by Americans on imports of foreign goods than by foreigners on exports of American goods.

This recording of credits, debits, surpluses, and deficits is done within a structure of sub-accounts of the overall balance of payments. These sub-accounts are the trade account, the services account, the transfers account, the capital account, and the official reserves account. Within these sub-accounts, four balances are particularly prominent or important — the trade balance, the current account balance, the overall non-official balance, and changes in the reserve account.

## Trade Account

The most widely known of the international balance of payments accounts is the trade account. This account records the monetary flows that take place in payment for the exports or imports of physical goods such as oil, aircraft, computers, wheat, textiles, footwear, steel, etc. It is this account that we hear referred to monthly in the context of the United States having a large trade deficit — i.e., US trade imports exceeding US trade exports, or Japan having a large trade surplus — i.e., Japanese trade exports exceeding Japanese trade imports.

## Services Account

A second category of the international balance of payments accounts is the services account. This account records the payments for international transactions involving various economic services, as opposed to goods. Some of the prominent items in this account are tourism, royalties on international licensing of technology, and fees for shipping services. The services account also records payments to and receipts from abroad of investment income, such as profits and interest. In contrast to its trade deficit, the United States has a sizeable services account surplus as a result of strengths in many economic service areas, such as banking and technology development.

## Transfers Account

A third category is the transfers account. This account refers to transfers of funds from economic entities in one country to entities in another for the purpose of extending aid or making a gift. The transfer account is further divided into official and private components. The main items included in the official component are extensions of foreign aid by governments. Not surprisingly, the United States has a deficit in its official transfer account, a result of foreign aid grants of the US Government. On the other side of the ledger, countries which for the most part receive foreign aid, such as Egypt, Israel, and, recently, Russia, have positive balances in their official transfer accounts to reflect the inflows of aid.

In the private transfers account, the main activity recorded is an international flow of funds called worker remittances — essentially the process of immigrant workers in one country sending money back home. At many US post offices on Saturday mornings, one can see this activity occur in the form of immigrants from Latin America buying postal money orders to mail home. The United States and many countries in Western Europe with large immigrant worker populations have negative balances in their private transfers accounts, while countries that have experienced heavy emigration of workers, like El Salvador, Mexico, Turkey, and Algeria, have surpluses in their private transfers account.

### The Current Account Balance

These three accounts — trade, services, and transfers — often are combined into a summary measure called the current account balance. This measure is thought by economists to be a better measure of the international economic performance of a country than the trade balance since it accounts for international payments for services and transfers as well as for trade. With these latter flows increasing in importance, it is more important than before to consider them, and hence to use the current account balance over the trade balance as a preferred indicator of international economic performance. In the case of the United States, the current account deficit is smaller than the trade deficit because of the large surplus in the US service accounts (see Figures 2-1 and 2-2).

**Figure 2-1  US Current Account Flows, 1997 ($ billions)**

| | |
|---|---|
| Exports of Goods | 673 |
| Imports of Goods | 870 |
| Trade Balance | -197 |
| | |
| Balance on Non-Investment Services | 85 |
| Balance on Investment Income | -11 |
| Services Balance | 74 |
| | |
| Net Transfers | -36 |
| | |
| Current Account Balance | -166 |

Source: Council of Economic Advisers, *Economic Report of the President, 1998.* January-September trend expressed at annual rate.

Figure 2-2 US Trade and Current Account Balances

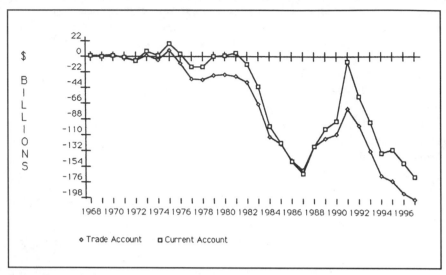

Source: Council of Economic Advisers, *Economic Report of the President, 1998.*

## Capital Account

Consideration of just the current account balance is not enough, however. With capital flows becoming even more sizeable and important than current account flows, it has become essential to also consider equally the capital account. Indeed, it has been in the capital account that nearly all the international financial crises of the 1990s, such as Europe in 1992, Mexico in 1994, East Asia in 1997, and Russia in 1998, have originated.

Capital flows are international flows of money related to domestic investors making new capital investments in a foreign country or to foreign investors making new investments into a country.

- When a country's businesses or investors make an investment in another country, the result is capital leaving the country — a capital outflow — that is recorded as a debit in the capital accounts.

- When a foreign business or investor makes a capital investment into a country, the result is capital coming into the country — a capital inflow — that is recorded as a credit in the country's capital accounts.

The capital account is divided into two parts — portfolio investment and direct investment. When a business or individual in one country makes a loan, deposits money in a bank, buys bonds, or buys non-controlling amounts of stock in another country, the transaction is recorded in the portfolio section of the non-official capital account. Examples of these transactions for the United States include US banks loaning money to South American businesses and governments (a US portfolio capital debit), Middle Eastern businesses and governments depositing their oil earnings in US banks (a US portfolio capital credit), Japanese investors buying US government and corporate bonds (US portfolio capital credit), and US mutual funds investing in foreign stock markets (US portfolio capital debit).

When a business, individual or government takes a major ownership interest in an economic activity in another country, either by starting a new business operation, by buying into an existing one, or by engaging in a joint venture with a foreign company, the transaction is recorded in the direct investment account, with investments of domestic businesses and investors in foreign countries being recorded as direct investment capital outflow debits and foreign investments in the domestic economy being recorded as direct investment capital inflow credits.

For the United States, actions that create direct investment capital inflows include the establishment of US auto assembly plants by Japanese automobile companies, purchases of small US technology companies by Japanese companies, and the buying into the Kiawah Island, South Carolina, resort development by the Kuwait Finance Corporation. Activities that result in US direct investment capital outflows include the ongoing building of factories in Mexico by US corporations.

In contrast to the deficit in its current account, the United States has run large surpluses in its non-official capital account over the past decade. In 1997, for example, a surplus of more than $100 billion was recorded, on capital inflows related to foreign investment in the United States of over $600 billion and capital outflows related to US investors investing overseas of over $400 billion. In effect, over this period, foreign investors made more portfolio and direct investments in the United States than US investors have made investments abroad.

### Official International Reserves Account

The final category in a country's international balance of payments accounts records changes in that country's holdings of official international reserves in the official capital or official reserve account. These official international reserves are financial assets held by the country's central bank that are readily acceptable by other countries' central banks as payment for international financial obligations.

These reserves are typically made up of foreign exchange, i.e. other countries' currencies, gold, and countries' allocations through the International Monetary Fund of something called special drawing rights (SDRs). The central bank's holdings of its own currency is not counted as official international reserves because this currency may not be, and for many countries is not, readily acceptable to settle financial obligations in foreign countries. For most countries, holding of foreign exchange comprises the majority of their official international reserves.

Countries' official international reserve holdings vary widely. In mid 1998, the United States had $60 billion, Germany had $80 billion, Japan had $205 billion, China had over $140 billion, and India had $24 billion.

The official international reserves section of a country's international balance of payments accounts relates to the other sections as a balance wheel. Specifically, when a country runs a combined balance of payments surplus in its current and capital accounts, it will accumulate reserves. When a country runs a combined balance of payments deficit in its current and capital accounts, it will lose reserves (see Figure 2-3). This reserve gain or loss also is connected with foreign exchange market intervention actions by the country's central bank, an issue discussed in Chapter 8. Figure 2-4 summarizes the components of the balance of payments accounts and provides examples of economic actions recorded in them.

### What the Balances and Imbalances Mean

In concluding our discussion of countries' international balance of payments accounts, it is important to examine the implications of a country running deficits or surpluses in its balance of payments. First of all, it is not possible for a country to run an imbalance in the entire account structure because of the balance wheel function of the official reserve accounts. As discussed above, a combined current and non-official capital accounts surplus is balanced by a rise in reserves, and a deficit by a fall in reserves.

It is possible, and even probable, however, for a country to run surpluses or deficits in other parts of the accounts. One must be careful, therefore, to correctly interpret the meaning and significance of imbalances in these accounts.

**Figure 2-3  Selected Countries: Relation between Current Account, Non-Official Capital Account, Changes in Official International Reserves ($ billions)**

|  | United States 1997 | Japan 1997 | Thailand 1996 | Thailand 1997 |
|---|---|---|---|---|
| Current Account Balance | -166 | 94 | -23 | -3 |
| Capital Account Balance | 167 | -88 | 25 | -15 |
| Changes in Official Reserves | Up 1 | Up 6 | Up 2 | Down 18 |

Source: International Monetary Fund, *International Financial Statistics*, August 1998.

**Figure 2-4  Summary of Components of Balance of Payments Accounts**

| Account | Economic Action Causing Credit | Economic Action Causing Debit |
|---|---|---|
| Trade | Export of Physical Goods | Import of Physical Goods |
| Services | Export of Economic Service | Import of Economic Service |
| Transfer | Receipt of Foreign Gift | Gift to Foreign Entity |
| Capital | Investment by Foreigners into Country | Investment by Domestic Entities Abroad |

- Very little significance should be attached to imbalances in individual parts of the balance of payments — trade, services, capital, etc. — if the imbalances are offset by opposite imbalances in other parts of the non-official accounts. Thus, the steady and large current account deficits that the United States ran in the 1980s created no financial crisis because these deficits were being almost completely offset by capital account surpluses.

- A problem does occur, however, if a country is incurring a combined deficit in its current and capital accounts. In this case, the combined deficit will mean that the country is steadily drawing down its official international reserves, a situation that obviously must come to an end at some point, at the latest when the country exhausts its reserves.

- On the other hand, the opposite situation — a combined surplus in the current and capital accounts — can continue longer because in this case the country is gaining reserves. This outcome occurred in the small island economy of Taiwan where over the course of the 1980s reserve holdings rose to near $100 billion because of ongoing combined current and capital account surpluses. However, allowing reserves to build up creates internal financial stresses that eventually cause problems.

- Finally, it is critical to note that rises and falls in reserves are closely associated with particular policy choices of countries' central banks to have fixed as opposed to floating exchange rates (see next section). Specifically, declines in reserves are an indication that central banks are engaging in explicit actions to hold up the value of the currency and increases in reserves are an indication that central banks are engaging in actions to hold down the value of the currency.

## Exchange Rates

A second measure of a country's international economic situation is the rate at which the country's currency exchanges for other currencies on foreign exchange markets, and whether this exchange rate is rising or falling. Exchange rates can be found in the business section of most major newspapers. In September 1998, for example, exchange rate tables showed the dollar to be exchangeable for 134 Japanese yen, 1.73 German marks, 1.42 Swiss francs, etc. (see Figure 2-5). These exchange rates meant that if you took $1000 to a bank or other firm that dealt in the foreign exchange market, you could receive in exchange something close to 134,000 yen, 1730 marks, and 1420 Swiss francs. You would not get exactly this amount because the bank would deduct a small amount for carrying out the exchange.

**Figure 2-5  Exchange Rates with US Dollar, September 1998**
**(Units of Foreign Currency Obtainable with One Dollar)**

| Japanese Yen | 134 | German Mark | 1.73 |
|---|---|---|---|
| French Franc | 5.64 | British Pound | 0.60 |
| Swiss Franc | 1.42 | Italian Lira | 1662 |
| Canada Dollar | 1.52 | Belgium Franc | 34.71 |
| Sweden Krona | 7.94 | Netherlands Guilder | 1.89 |

Source: Various newspapers, September, 1998.

### Appreciation and Depreciation

In using exchange rates as a measure of a country's economic situation, however, it is not only what exchange rates are that is of interest to economists, but also what they are doing — i.e., is the currency rising in value, what economists call appreciating, or falling in value, what economists call depreciating.

Appreciation of a currency means that the exchange rate has moved in a direction that will allow one unit of the domestic currency to buy more units of foreign currency. Using the exchange rates provided above as a starting point, an appreciation of the dollar would result in rates like 140 yen, 1.84 marks, and 1.60 Swiss francs. Conversely, depreciation of a currency means the domestic currency will buy fewer units of foreign currencies — i.e., exchange rates for the dollar of 70 yen, 1.24 marks, and 1.00 Swiss francs, for example. A large, rapid depreciation often is called a currency collapse. Finally, it is important to remember that when one currency appreciates against another currency, an opposite movement will have occurred with the second currency — i.e., a depreciation of the dollar against the yen means an appreciation of the yen against the dollar.

## Floating and Fixed Exchange Rates

Exchange rates can be floating or fixed. A floating exchange rate means that private sector supply and demand forces in foreign exchange markets are the sole determinants of exchange rates. Governments and central banks are not declaring a particular exchange rate as the proper rate and not taking actions to fix the value of the exchange rate at that rate. Since 1971, the United States has had for the most part a floating exchange rate in which the dollar's value is determined by what economists call market forces. Chapter 6 discusses exactly how these forces determine exchange rates.

A fixed exchange rate means that the country's central bank, perhaps in coordination with other countries' central banks, has decided the exchange rate for the currency should be fixed at some specific rate and is prepared to take actions necessary to maintain this exchange rate (more on these actions in Chapter 8).

At present, a major set of fixed exchange rates exists among 11 European currencies in an arrangement called the European Monetary System; the German mark and French franc have a fixed rate with each other, for example. This fixed exchange rate system is a prelude to a replacement of these 11 currencies by a single European currency called the Euro. Other currencies are pegged to the US dollar, such as Argentina's currency, and others to other major currencies.

Sometimes, as occurred in Europe in late 1992 and early 1993, and in Mexico in 1994, economic pressures force these fixed rates to be changed. Changes of fixed exchange rates in a downward direction are called devaluations, in an upward direction, revaluations. Economic pressures also can force fixed exchange rates to become floating, as occurred with many East Asian currencies in 1997 and 1998.

## Meaning of Exchange Rate Movements

Unlike real GDP growth rates, inflation rates, and unemployment rates, where a lower or higher rate tends to have a clear value judgment attached to it — i.e., a high inflation rate is bad and a low unemployment rate is good — appreciation or depreciation, or revaluation or devaluation, of a currency is ambiguous in terms of its goodness or badness. A depreciation of a currency tends to carry a negative connotation with it — "Our currency is worth less!" — but in fact can have a number of positive benefits, such as boosting exports by making domestic products less expensive to foreign buyers (again see Chapter 6). However, currency collapses are always harmful to a country's economy.

## Trends in the Dollar's Exchange Rate

For the first 25 years of the post World War II period, the dollar remained stable in its international value, chiefly because the dollar and most other major currencies were in a fixed exchange rate system called the Bretton

Woods system. Since 1971, however, the dollar has floated, and private sector decisions in the international economy have been allowed to set the value of the dollar without major interference from governments and central banks. During that period, the dollar has generally depreciated in value against many major currencies (see Figure 2-6), but on a number of occasions has appreciated also, including in 1996-98.

**Figure 2-6  Exchange Rate of US Dollar with Japanese Yen and German Mark**

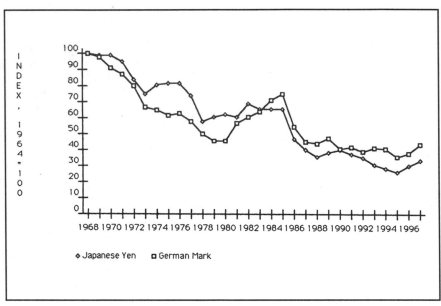

Source: Council of Economic Advisers, *Economic Report of the President, 1998.*

## Summary

1.  Two measures are most commonly used to portray a country's international economic situation.

2.  The international balance of payments shows the balance of financial flows into and out of a country's economy. These accounts record as credits to the accounts flows of money into the country and as debits flows of money out of the country.

3.  The international balance of accounts is divided into a number of sub-accounts — the trade account, the services account, the transfer account, the current account, the non-official capital account, and the official reserves account.

4. When credits exceed debits for a particular account or the overall balance of payments, a surplus is said to occur; when debits exceed credits, a deficit results.

5. Being in surplus or deficit in particular parts of these accounts does have implications, but neither is as clearly good or bad as much commentary suggests, although an overall balance of payments surplus or deficit is significant.

6. The exchange rates of a country's currency with other currencies — and whether these exchange rates are appreciating or depreciating — also are used as a measure of its international economic situation.

7. Like balance of payments surpluses or deficits, both appreciation and depreciation have implications, but neither is uniformly good or bad. A depreciation, for example, makes a country's imports cost more, but, on the other hand, makes its exports more competitive.

8. Some countries fix their exchange rates with other countries through actions of their central bank. Other countries allow their exchange rates to float according to private market pressures. The US dollar by and large floats.

# 3 | Basic Principles of Economics

While the focus of this book is on nations' overall economic performances, covering such "in the news" economic concepts as recession, inflation, unemployment, interest rates, trade balances, exchange rate movements, budget deficits, and the money supply, it is important to first examine a few basic economic principles that underlie all of the economic trends we read about.

## Economic Goals

All societies have economic goals that form the basis for economic activity. Specifically, societies and their individual members desire to ever expand their level of material satisfaction — i.e. societies want to consume ever higher levels of economic products. Some of the products that societies desire are goods — such tangible items as cars, appliances, clothing, food, and shelter. Others are services — such as medical care, education, transportation and financial services.

In assessing economic goals of societies with regard to consumption of these economic products, economists believe that societies' desires for economic products are insatiable. That is, there can never be enough economic products produced to fully satisfy, although there may be occasions where a society gets all it wants of one particular product. Thus, one of the key concepts around which economic analysis is built is insatiable wants of societies for economic products.

## Economic Constraints

If there were no constraints on the ability of societies to obtain economic products, there would be no problem, no need for economics, and no job for me, at least as an economist. However, in the real world, the economic products that satisfy these material wants are not freely and unboundedly available. Indeed, there are severe constraints on the extent to which they are available, because they are produced with economic resources which are limited in their availability.

Identification of the economic resources used to produce economic products will illustrate their limited nature.

- One category of economic resources used to produce economic products is labor—i.e., people working. This resource is limited by the number of people able and willing to work. In the United States, while there are about 137 million people in the labor force, the number is nonetheless limited.

- A second economic resource is what economists call human capital — essentially the amount of skill, education, and training that an individual worker or the labor force at large has. It too is limited, often severely. For example, there are shortages of certain engineering and computer technician skills in the US economy, which in turn limits the ability of the US economy to produce products using those skills.

- A third category of economic resources is physical capital, i.e. items made for the purpose, not of direct consumption, but for their usefulness in producing other products. Examples of physical capital include factories, capital equipment, commercial buildings, roads, ports — anything that has been constructed for the purpose of creating or facilitating production. While each year economies get more physical capital through capital formation, or investment, clearly there is not unlimited physical capital available to the US or any other economy.

- In today's world, an especially important category of economic resources is technology — new products and production processes such as wide bodied jet aircraft, personal computers, networked computers, advanced telecommunication systems, and bio-production processes. Indeed, economists now rate this economic resource as one of the most important of all types of economic resources. It is not unlimited in supply. For example, it would be great for meeting economies need for energy if sunlight could be easily turned into electricity, even on a cloudy day. Unfortunately, the technology that can do so does not yet exist.

- In contrast to the resource of technology, which is growing in importance, a resource which is declining in importance, but is nonetheless limited in supply relative to what economies could use, is natural resources. When economists refer to natural resources, they mean items useful in production that have been provided by nature — crude oil, iron ore, bauxite, copper ore, water, forests (unless the forest has been planted by a forestry products company, in which case it could easily be called physical capital), arable land, to name only a few. For a variety of reasons more fully discussed in Chapter 12, the world economy is now less reliant on natural resources, but nonetheless has less of these resources than it could make use of, and occasionally actually has shortages of certain resources, such as occurred when political events caused shortfalls in world oil supplies in the 1970s.

- Another important economic resource is financial capital, not money per se, but organizations and institutions such as banks, stock markets, venture capitalists, that create a stable, enabling financial environment. The Asian economic crises of 1997-98 revealed major shortfalls in those countries' financial capital resources.

The final economic resource that economists identify — and one that is often overlooked, but is perhaps the most essential — is the ability to organize the other economic resources in a way that results in useful economic products being produced. In a market, capitalist economy like the United States, this resource is embodied in the men and women who organize and run businesses and is traditionally called entrepreneurship. In socialist economies in which the government owns many of the business activities, this resource is embodied — albeit much less efficiently — in the men and women who manage these state enterprises for the government. This resource too is limited. Figure 3-1 summarizes these general categories of economic resources.

**Figure 3-1  Summary of Economic Resources**

| Category of Resources | Real World Examples |
|---|---|
| Labor | Unskilled workers |
| Human Capital | Engineers, technicians, scientists, inventors |
| Physical Capital | Factories, assembly lines, roads, ports |
| Natural Resources | Crude oil, iron ore, coal, forests |
| Technology | Computers, telecommunication, bioproduction |
| Financial Capital | Banks, stock markets, venture capitalists |
| Entrepreneurship | Owners and senior managers of businesses |

## Economic Systems

Faced with these tensions between the unlimited economic wants of their citizens and the limited economic resources they have to produce the products that meet these wants, nations and societies have organized their economic systems in a wide variety of ways. The most pervasive and notable of these systems are capitalism and socialism, the latter of which communism is a variant.

Capitalism is an economic system in which the main factors of production — technology, physical capital, financial capital, etc. — are owned by private businesses, often called corporations. Within capitalism, however, wide variations exist.

- Some capitalist countries might be called government-directed capitalism. In these countries, frequently found in East Asia, the government, through subsidies, credit access, and general guidance, play a major role in economic decisions.

- Other capitalist countries, perhaps called government-impeded capitalism, and found frequently in Europe, have private corporations as the main producers of economic products, but impede their activities through high taxes and regulations.

- Finally, exemplified by the United States and Britain, some capitalists more closely approach what is called free market capitalism. In these countries, the government does not direct economic activity and does not have high taxes and regulations, at least by comparison.

Economists generally define two types of socialism.

- Market Socialism is a system in which the government owns large amounts of the nation's productive resources through state-owned enterprises, but, at least in theory, allow these enterprises to function as independent economic entities. The philosophy behind this system is that these state enterprises will be operated as private businesses but profits will go to the government for the benefit of society at large rather than to private owners. Until Prime Minister Margaret Thatcher restructured the British economy in the early 1980s, Britain was a prominent example of market socialism, with such firms as British Rail, British Steel, British Coal, and British Air all owned by the British government. Today, most examples of market socialist economic systems are found in the so-called Third World — Africa, the Middle East, South Asia, and Latin America.

- Planned Socialism is a system that is most often associated with communism and which predominated in the former Soviet Union and Eastern Europe. In this system, not only does the government own the producing economic resources, but also directs them centrally. The USSR, for example, guided its economy with a rigid, comprehensive economic plan. Today, because of the economic reform efforts that have swept the world, few planned socialism economic systems remain, with the most prominent remaining examples being Cuba and North Korea. Figure 3-2 summarizes these alternative economic systems.

As is evident from what has occurred in the world in the past half-decade, socialism is dying as a viable economic system. As mentioned in the previous paragraph, almost all planned socialist systems have shifted to another system, probably somewhere between market socialism and consumer-oriented capitalism. Eastern Europe and China fall into this category. Additionally, many market socialist countries have shifted in the direction of capitalism. The aforementioned Britain is one example, but many Third World countries have also made the shift — like Mexico, Argentina, and Chile in Latin America and Thailand, India, and Indonesia in Asia.

#### Figure 3-2 Alternative Economic Systems

| System | Characteristics | Examples |
|---|---|---|
| Government-directed Capitalism | private ownership of productive resources; government actions that directly shape economic decisions | East Asia |
| Government-impeded Capitalism | private ownership of productive resources; government taxes and regulations that impede private economic activity | Continental Western Europe |
| Free Market Capitalism | private ownership of productive resources; no government direction of economic decisions and lower taxes and regulations | United States, Britain |
| Market Socialism | government owns productive resources; each government enterprise operates as business | South America, Middle East, Africa |
| Planned Socialism | government owns productive resources and directs them centrally | Former USSR, North Korea and Cuba today |

## Economic Choices

Whether the economic system is capitalism or socialism, the tension created by unlimited economic wants and limited economic resources forces each economy and society to make choices in the economic arena. Simply put, since a society cannot have all of the economic products it wants, it must decide which it will have and which it will not have. Economists generally discuss this issue of choosing under what is called the basic economic questions of societies, and define three main choices that economies make with regard to dealing with the tension between unlimited wants and limited resources.

One decision is *what* products to produce, including how much of each. Since not enough economic resources exist to produce all products in unlimited quantities, a decision must be made as to what products to produce and in what quantities.

Planned economic systems like the former USSR made these decisions in a very explicit, centralized way, while market economies like the United States make this choice through the de-centralized workings of markets. In a market economy, the major economic actor affecting its outcome is the consumer, by the products he or she buys or does not buy in a attempt to achieve the highest possible level of material satisfaction. However, even in a market economy like the United States, the government affects the what choice through its taxation and spending decisions. For instance, taxation of a product raises its price and discourages its consumption, while spending money on a product increases the demand for it and boosts its production (see also Chapter 7).

A second economic choice is *how* to produce. Since unlimited supplies of economic resources are not available for use in the production process, choices must be made among the limited quantities of resources available. In a market economy like the United States, this decision is made primarily by businesses run by entrepreneurs. These businesses invariably choose the set of resources for producing a product that yields the least cost method of production. As with the what choice, however, while businesses are the primary influence in the how choice, numerous other factors — including the actions of government (see again Chapter 7) — also exert influence, by raising or lowering the costs of resources and thereby shifting which resources businesses wish to use.

In today's globalized economy (see Chapter 12), an important offshoot of the how decision is *where*. That is, today a company not only has the choice of using labor or capital to produce its product, but where to use this labor or capital, in the United States, Mexico, the Caribbean, Southeast Asia, etc.

The third basic economic choice economists define, and the one for which it is hard to establish a primary actor, is the *for whom* decision. In a market economy this question is answered through the following sequence of activities: individuals acquire products in a market economy by using money to buy them; individuals obtain money from receiving income; individuals acquire income by having and selling economic resources they own. Therefore, the people who receive the products in a market economy are those which own valuable economic resources — the ability to work, a particular human capital skill, a company, an oil field, an invention, particular entrepreneurial talents, etc. The people who have a lot of these resources have high incomes, secure many economic products, and are called the rich.

Unfortunately, if an individual has few economic resources, he or she will receive little income and in turn will have little ability to obtain the products of the economy. In common language, they will be poor. Because of this latter outcome, the United States and many other countries put in place policies that provide these individuals supplements to their incomes in the form of income assistance payments. These payments are discussed further in Chapter 7.

## Supply, Demand, Price: The Main Tools of Economic Analysis

In a capitalist market economic system like that of the United States, and indeed in most any country in today's world, economists base their analysis of trends on the concepts of supply, demand, and price in these markets. Indeed, with these basic concepts — supply, demand, price, and their interaction — modified to the specific circumstances of the economic trends being examined, all questions in economics can be fundamentally answered.

These supply and demand forces, which drive all market economic performance and which will be used repeatedly in this book to better understand national and international economic trends, work on the basis of a few key principles.

- In each market, there is a demand that consists of certain groups purchasing the product or products. This demand rises or falls in response to changes in factors which determine how much of the product purchasers wish to buy.

- In each market, there is supply that consists of other groups placing the product on the market for sale. Supply rises or falls in response to changes in a different set of factors which determine how much of the product suppliers are able and willing to place on the market.

- These demand and supply relationships interact with each other through the price of the product to produce shifts in the behavior of the participants that transmits initial shifts in demand or supply to the other.

- Increases in demand — caused by a greater ability or willingness to purchase products — pull up prices and through the higher prices produce increases in output; decreases in demand — driven by drops in ability or willingness to make purchases — lead to lower prices and decreases in output.

- Increases in supply — created by increases in economic resources or increases in producers' willingness to use economic resources — cause more abundant supply and lower prices that induce increases in demand; decreases in supply — created by negative developments in economic resources or the willingness to use them — increase prices and lead to decreases in demand.

These supply-demand relationships and their interactions can be represented in graphical form, as in Figure 3-3. In this figure, the horizontal axis measures the physical amount of the product supplied and demanded and the vertical axis measures the price of the product. The demand representation slopes down to suggest, as seems likely, that a lower price for a product will induce more demand for it. The supply representation slopes upward to suggest, as economists believe likely, that if the price of a product rises, producers will be willing to put more of it on the market.

Equilibrium in the market occurs where there is neither excess demand for the product — a shortage — which would occur if the price were lower than equilibrium, nor excess supply of the product — a surplus — which would occur if the price were higher than equilibrium. In other words, in a given market, price, consumption, and production tend toward a point where supply equals demand, graphically represented by where the supply and demand lines intersect.

**Figure 3-3 Basic Concepts of Supply and Demand, Graphical Representation**

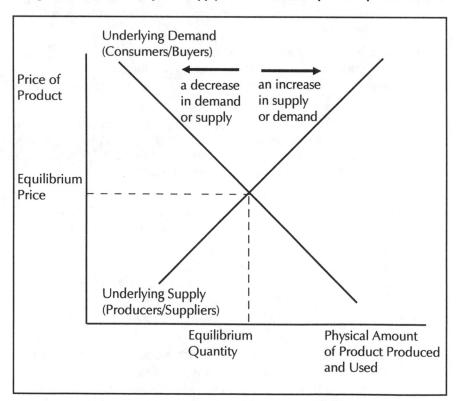

To use this graphical framework to assess impacts of economic trends, the supply and demand curves are shifted in response to events or factors which cause supply or demand to increase or decrease. For increases in supply or demand, the lines are shifted to the right; for decreases in supply or demand, they are shifted to the left.

As an example of how to use the framework, visualize Figure 3-3 as representing the market for oil. Then consider the impact on the supply of oil of a major drop in world oil supplies, as occurred in 1979-80 due to the revolution in the Persian Gulf country of Iran. This event would lead to a substantial drop in oil supply, a leftward shift in the oil market supply line, higher oil prices, and lower demand for oil — exactly what occurred between 1978 and 1981 when the Iranian Revolution caused a major drop in the availability of oil, oil prices rose from $12 to $35 per barrel and oil use fell by some 5 million barrels a day. Conversely, after 1981, as oil demand fell, in part in response to the earlier higher prices, and oil supplies began to rise again, oil prices fell.

To use the supply and demand framework to assess the functioning of a capitalist, market economy:

- define the market with regard to the product being examined and the demand, supply, and price in that market;

- delineate the determinants of supply and demand and how supply and demand respond to changes in these determinants;

- use the framework to assess the impact on the market of shifts in underlying factors of supply or demand, as with the oil market in the preceding paragraph.

In the next chapter, we will use these concepts and principles to build a supply and demand framework to examine how recession, expansion, and inflation trends are determined in a national economy like that of the United States.

## Summary

1. While this book is primarily about performance of overall economic systems like that of the United States, it is important to begin with an examination of the basic forces that drive economic phenomena.

2. This examination begins with a recognition that all societies desire consumption of economic goods and services and that this desire is unlimited.

3. In contrast to this unlimited desire for economic products, the ability to produce these products is limited, because the economic resources with which economic products are made are limited in availability. While a given country may have many economic resources — labor, human capital, physical capital,

financial capital, technology, natural resources, and entrepreneurship — no society has them in unlimited abundance.

4. As a result of unlimited economic wants but limited economic
resources to produce the goods to satisfy these wants, societies
must make economic choices. Economists generally group these
choices into: what and how much to produce, how and where to
produce, and to whom the products are distributed.

5. Some societies, like the former USSR, make these choices in a
centralized fashion under the auspices of the government, but
now, most societies make them in a de-centralized way through
the operation of capitalist, market forces.

6. For these economic systems, economists have devised a simple,
very effective framework for analyzing the impact of various economic events on economic trends. This framework is called
supply and demand.

7. Supply and demand analysis assesses economic trends and behavior by examining the impact of various events on supply or
demand, examining how initial shifts in supply or demand affect
price, and then examining how supply or demand respond to the
changes in price.

8. With this framework, nearly all economic phenomena can be
examined, including all of the key economic performance measures to be looked at in this book.

# 4 | Causes of Recession, Expansion, and Inflation

Building on the last chapter, we will attempt to gain better understanding of causes of recession, expansion, and inflation through examination of a country's economy as an aggregate market for goods and services. In this framework, aggregate supply and aggregate demand are the primary driving forces in economic performance. Aggregate supply is the ability and willingness of the country's businesses to put product on the market, given a variety of underlying factors, while aggregate demand is the ability and willingness of the country's buyers to purchase products, i.e. engage in spending, and is also dependent on a variety of factors.

Figure 4-1 provides a graphical representation of this economy-wide supply and demand framework. In this framework, the downward slope of the aggregate demand line represents the fact that if the overall level of prices rises, then consumers will make fewer purchases as a result of higher prices reducing real incomes and purchasing power. The upward slope of the aggregate supply line represents economists' belief that if product prices rise — i.e. the overall price level rises — then producers will be willing and able to put more product on the market.

The steadily steeper slope for the aggregate supply curve represents another belief of economists, that as more and more resources are utilized, as would be the case as real GDP rises, the supply response becomes increasingly smaller as the economy moves closer to full employment. Eventually, at full employment or full capacity, it becomes impossible to produce any more products, no matter how great the demand, and, at this point, the aggregate supply curve becomes vertical.

## Aggregate Supply and Demand and Recession, Expansion, and Inflation

Given this representation, connections between aggregate supply and demand and trends in real GDP and inflation are as follows.

- Recession is caused either by declines in spending / aggregate demand or by declines in aggregate supply. Expansions are caused

by the reverse, rises in spending / aggregate demand or by rises in aggregate supply.

- Inflation is caused either by increases in spending / aggregate demand or by decreases in aggregate supply. Inflation is lowered by opposite shifts in aggregate demand or supply.

**Figure 4-1  Aggregate Demand and Aggregate Supply, Graphical Representation**

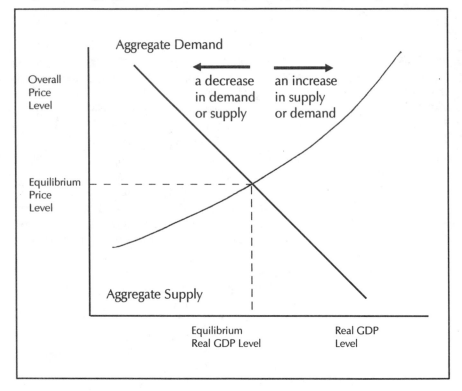

One can examine these principles graphically by shifting the aggregate demand and supply curves in Figure 4-1 in appropriate directions and verifying the new equilibrium levels of real GDP and inflation are as indicated. For example, if aggregate demand rises, in graphical terms the aggregate demand curve shifts to the right, producing a new equilibrium level of higher real GDP and higher prices or inflation. Or, if aggregate supply falls, the aggregate supply curve shifts to the left, producing a new equilibrium level of real GDP and prices or inflation that are, respectively, lower and higher than initially.

However, understanding these relationships between aggregate demand, aggregate supply, real GDP and inflation gives us only part of the information needed. It also is necessary to understand what causes increases and decreases in aggregate supply and aggregate demand in the first place. It is to that task that we now turn.

# Causes of Changes in Spending and Aggregate Demand

Aggregate demand changes, and in turn affects real GDP and inflation, when the spending decisions of consumers, businesses, or foreign economic agents change and when government policies that affect these decisions change.

## Consumers

One main group affecting an economy's aggregate demand is consumers, like you and I, who make personal consumption expenditures to purchase goods and services to satisfy personal wants. When these expenditures rise or fall, aggregate demand rises or falls.

These personal consumption expenditures are heavily determined by four factors:

- consumer incomes, with higher incomes causing higher expenditures as consumers take advantage of increased income to buy more products, and lower incomes producing opposite effects;

- interest rates, with lower interest rates causing more personal consumption expenditures, especially on "big ticket" items like automobiles, durable goods and housing that requires borrowing money to make the purchases, and higher interest rates reducing consumer spending;

- taxes on consumers, with higher taxes reducing consumption by reducing "take-home" earnings, and lower taxes increasing consumption; and

- consumer expectations about the future, with a more optimistic view leading to increased personal consumption, and a pessimistic view cutting consumer expenditures.

The overall price level or inflation also affects consumer spending, but with an uncertain impact. On the one hand, higher prices or inflation can cause lower consumption expenditures as consumers are forced by the reduction in their real incomes to cut spending. However, if the higher prices cause consumers to expect even higher prices in the future, they may accelerate their purchases to beat the expected price increases. Conversely, lower overall prices will give consumers more real income, which will enable them to purchase more consumer items, but if they expect even lower prices in the future, they may hold back on present spending. In the US and most other economies, these personal consumption expenditures account for the largest but a relatively stable part of aggregate demand.

## Domestic Businesses

A second group that impacts heavily on overall spending in an economy is domestic businesses. In terms of aggregate demand, businesses demand a particular type of output called investment goods, goods they use to expand or upgrade their productive capacity. Examples of these goods are a new computer system, a new assembly line, a new office building, a new fleet of airliners.

Like consumption expenditures, when business investment rises or falls, aggregate demand rises or fall, and, like consumption, business investment is driven by several underlying factors:

- the level of business profits, with higher profits raising investment by making available more funds to finance investment, and lower profits reducing investment;

- interest rates, with lower interest rates increasing investment by reducing the cost of borrowing funds to finance the investment, and higher interest rates lowering investment;

- the closeness of production to capacity levels, with being closer to capacity causing more investment as business invests to be able to have more capacity to meet the demand for its products, and having excess capacity reducing investment;

- the direction of change in aggregate demand, with rising aggregate demand causing more investment to meet the additional demand, and falling demand reducing investment;

- taxes and regulations on businesses, with more taxes or regulations reducing investment by making it harder or less profitable to carry out business activities, and less taxes or regulations generally stimulating investment; and

- business expectations about the future, with business investment likely to be stimulated by favorable expectations such as for lower costs of production, lower taxes, lower interest rates, and depressed by unfavorable expectations.

The level of business investment demand only accounts for about a fifth of total US aggregate demand and larger percentages in other countries. However, because it is highly variable, it is a major factor in changes in countries' overall real GDP and inflation trends.

## Foreign Economic Actors

A third determinant of a country's aggregate demand, growing in importance in today's world, is foreign economic actors, who impact directly in two ways, and indirectly, but no less importantly, in another. First, foreign actors add to aggregate demand when they demand domestic products through purchases of exports. Second, they subtract from aggregate demand when they successfully penetrate the domestic market through their exports (domestic imports).

Given these connections, a given country's aggregate demand, and in turn its real GDP and inflation, will be boosted by increased foreign economic activity which will stimulate more of the first country's exports, and will be reduced by foreign economic recession. Conversely, increased foreign economic competitiveness will enable foreign producers to be better able to penetrate the domestic market, in turn reducing aggregate demand, real GDP, and inflation, while lower levels of foreign competition will cause a country's aggregate demand for its own goods to be higher.

Another way in which foreign economic actors affect aggregate demand is through their investment decisions. Specifically, if they choose to invest more in a given country's economy, the inflow of financial capital will stimulate consumption and investment. Conversely, if they reduce investment in the country's economy, aggregate demand will be reduced. For the United States, and most other countries, this factor is increasingly important, given the globalization of financial markets.

Both of these factors played significant roles in the 1997–98 financial crises in East Asia.

- The crises began with large capital outflows that led to major recessions in many East Asian countries.

- As these countries' real GDPs fell, so did their imports, leading to falls in exports and GDPs in other countries, including the United States.

### The Government and the Central Bank

The final groups which impact on aggregate demand are the country's government and the central bank. They impact in several ways. First, government adds to aggregate demand by the amount of spending it does. Some of this addition is direct when the government carries out its purchases of economic goods and services — military equipment, teachers' services, materials to build highways, general supplies, etc. Some of the addition is indirect and occurs through transfer payments the government makes to certain groups — social security benefits, unemployment compensation, welfare benefits, etc. — which boost incomes and cause increased personal consumption spending.

In contrast, the government reduces aggregate demand through taxes, which cut the disposable income of consumers and businesses and lowers their spending. A reversal of these government actions — i.e., a reduction in government spending or an increase in taxes — has opposite effects. The borrowing that occurs when the government runs a budget deficit also affects aggregate demand by pushing up interest rates, with the higher interest rates lowering spending and demand.

Countries' central banks also affect aggregate demand through monetary policy. An expansionary monetary policy — a larger money supply and lower interest rates — leads to higher aggregate demand because of the lower interest rates and easier credit the policy creates. A contractionary monetary policy has reverse effects on aggregate demand.

Because the role of government spending and taxation — what economists call fiscal policy — and the monetary policy of the central bank are so important in the performance of real GDP and inflation, we re-examine these issues in more detail in Chapters 7 and 8. Figure 4-2 summarizes key economic groups and how they impact on aggregate demand in a country's economy.

**Figure 4-2   Key Groups That Determine Aggregate Demand
and Factors Affecting Their Behavior**

| Group | Connection to Aggregate Demand | Causes of Increases to Aggregate Demand |
|---|---|---|
| Consumers | Consumption Spending | Lower Interest Rates<br>Higher Incomes<br>More Optimism<br>Lower Consumer Taxes |
| Businesses | Investment | Lower Interest Rates<br>Higher Profits<br>Closeness to Capacity<br>Higher Expected Profit<br>Lower Business Taxes |
| Government | Spending and Taxes | Higher Spending<br>Lower Taxes |
| Central Bank | Money Supply Changes | Higher Money Supply |
| Foreign Economic Actors | Trade and Investment | Foreign Economic Expansion<br>Less Foreign Competitiveness<br>More Capital Inflows |

*Note: Decreases in aggregate demand are produced by opposites of these trends.*

## Aggregate Demand, Real GDP, and Inflation in the Real World

A number of real world examples can be given to show how these interactions among the determinants of aggregate demand, real GDP, and inflation, have actually operated. As you read these examples, it may be useful to refer back to the figures in Chapter 1 to see how real world trends played out in these situations.

- When US interest rates rose to very high levels in the early 1980s, the impact was to lower personal consumption expenditures and business investment, reduce aggregate demand and to lead to a significant recession — drop in real GDP — and a drop in inflation, as this framework would predict.

- When Saddam Hussein invaded Kuwait in 1990, consumer confidence plunged. In turn, consumers severely cut back on their spending, lowering aggregate demand, and contributed to the US recession of early 1991.

- In 1997–98, low interest rates, low inflation, and strong consumer and business confidence contributed to sharp increases in aggregate demand and strong real GDP growth.

To summarize, trends in aggregate demand are a major determinant of changes in real GDP and inflation. When aggregate demand in an economy rises, due to increases in one of the categories of spending — consumer spending, business investment, government purchases or transfers, or net foreign demand — the result is a higher level of real GDP, but also higher inflation. When aggregate demand decreases, it produces lower real GDP and lower inflation.

In turn, numerous events cause changes in aggregate demand. Aggregate demand is increased by events such as lower interest rates, foreign economic expansion, higher incomes, and higher government transfer payments. In contrast, events that lower aggregate demand include pessimistic outlooks for the future, higher government taxes, and a decline in the competitiveness of the domestic economy. Figure 4-3 summarizes connections from changes in determinants of aggregate demand through aggregate demand to changes in real GDP and inflation.

## Causes of Changes in Aggregate Supply

The other, and equally important, side of the aggregate demand and supply analytical framework is aggregate supply. To repeat the earlier definition, aggregate supply can best be described as the overall, underlying ability and willingness of business producers in an economy to put product on the market place. When businesses put more product on the market, aggregate supply has increased; when they put less, aggregate supply has decreased

This willingness and, especially, ability, is not unchanging over the level of real GDP, but, as briefly discussed earlier, is reduced the closer the economy is to capacity or full employment. In other words, as an economy gets close to capacity, the ability of business to add additional output is reduced because at full employment there are few unused inputs with which to add additional output. It is for this reason that the graphical representation of aggregate supply turns upward at higher levels of real GDP in Figure 4-1. What this graph illustrates is the fact that increases in demand when real GDP is low or in recession will likely not be very inflationary, but increases in demand when real GDP is high or in an economic boom situation will be very inflationary.

**Figure 4-3  Connections among Changes in Determinants,
Aggregate Demand and Real GDP and Inflation**

lower interest rates
higher incomes
higher consumer confidence
higher business confidence
higher profits
higher expected profits
lower taxes
increased exports
decreased foreign competition
increased capital inflows
              Lead to: higher aggregate demand
                    Which leads to: higher real GDP
                          higher inflation

higher interest rates
lower incomes
lower consumer confidence
lower business confidence
lower profits
lower expected profits
higher taxes
deceased exports
increased foreign competition
decreased capital inflows
              Lead to: lower aggregate demand
                    Which leads to: lower real GDP
                          lower inflation

In addition to being influenced by how close the economy is to capacity, aggregate supply also is affected by numerous other factors. Any events or trends that make production easier or businesses more willing to produce will lead to increases in aggregate supply and changes that make it harder to produce or businesses less willing to produce will decrease aggregate supply.

- Prices are highly significant, with higher prices leading to more supply, since at a higher price the potential profit will be greater and more costly production processes can have their costs covered more easily.

- Availability of production inputs also play a key role, with a greater availability leading to more supply, by making it easier for producers to obtain the inputs they need to increase output.

- Prices of production inputs are similarly important, with a lower price leading to greater supply, by making it less expensive for producers to obtain inputs they need.

- Taxes and regulations on a nation's businesses impact heavily, with less of either leading to more supply, by reducing, in both cases, what businesses in effect treat as another input cost;

- The productivity or technology of the business also is key, with improvements leading to more supply by making it possible to get more production out of a given number of inputs.

- Particularly over the longer run, the amount of business investment in the economy plays an important role, with more investment leading to more supply as the higher investment provides the business with more productive capital with which to increase production.

- The degree of competition, whether domestic or foreign, also obviously impacts on aggregate supply, with greater competition resulting in greater aggregate supply.

- Finally, a currency collapse creates a drop in aggregate supply in the country experiencing the collapse by making imported inputs more expensive and less available.

Opposite trends in these determinants lead to reductions in aggregate supply. Graphically, events leading to increases in aggregate supply will shift aggregate supply curve to the right, and events leading to decreases in aggregate supply will shift aggregate supply curve to the left.

To make these abstract concepts more tangible, some real world examples of shifts in determinants of aggregate supply and the impacts on aggregate supply, real GDP and inflation can be given. Again, referring back to the figures in Chapter 1 will be useful in seeing what actually happened to real GDP and inflation in the face of these supply-side events.

- The two so-called Oil Price Shocks of 1974-75 and 1979-80 were examples of reduced input availability / higher input costs. The predicted result would be for a drop in aggregate supply and lower real GDP and higher inflation, both of which turned out to be true, with the United States and other industrialized countries suffering recessions and high inflation following the rise in oil prices.

- In the United States in the early 1980s, then-President Ronald Reagan instituted what was called "supply-side" economics, essentially a cut in government taxes on and regulation of business. The predicted result would be an increase in US aggregate supply, higher real GDP, and lower inflation, which turned out to occur, with US real growth being the highest it had been in over a decade and inflation slowing down.

- In the 1990s, one of the reasons that Russia had high inflation even while real GDP fell was that the economic reforms badly damaged the ability of the Russian economic system to get products to market — in effect, a reduction in aggregate supply which simultaneously produced lower output and higher inflation.

- An example of the relationship among closeness to capacity, aggregate supply, real GDP, and inflation occurred in the US economy in the late 1960s when several years of strong real GDP growth brought the economy closer and closer to capacity and led to steady increases in the inflation rate.

- As a final example, in Indonesia in 1998, the 80 percent decline in the value of the rupiah — a currency collapse — led to 60 percent inflation and a 15 percent drop in real GDP.

To summarize, when aggregate supply in an economy increases, the economy experiences faster growth in real GDP and lower inflation. When aggregate supply decreases, slower growth in real GDP, maybe even recession, and higher inflation will be the result. Changes in aggregate supply in turn are driven by changes in factors which affect ease and profitability of putting product into the market place.

Events that will cause higher profitability and increases in aggregate supply include improvements in productivity and technology and lower prices for production inputs. Events that will cause lower profitability and decreases in aggregate supply include increased government taxation, regulation of business, and reduced availability of production inputs. Also, because of differences in aggregate supply responses when the economy is in recession versus when it is near full employment, an economy will be more inflation prone near full employment than in or just after a recession. Figure 4-4 summarizes relationships among determinants of aggregate supply, aggregate supply, and real GDP and inflation.

## The Importance of Expectations

A final topic that needs discussed with regard to performance of real GDP and inflation in an economy is the role of expectations. In effect, the behavior of economic actors — consumers, business, etc. — is affected not only by what is going on today but by what is expected to go on in the future, and an expectation of a future event that will impact economically will cause a change in present behavior and thereby cause a change in real GDP and/or inflation, even before the event has occurred.

For example, if business expects tax rates to fall in the future and, in turn, their after-tax profits to rise, they likely will begin investing in anticipation today. This reaction will cause an increase in aggregate demand — the increased investment spending — and aggregate supply — the addition of the investment to business production capacities — and lead to a rise in real GDP without much additional inflation. A good part of the late 1980s investment boom in Mexico was a result of this process, with much of the boom beginning before the Mexican investment laws actually changed in anticipation the laws would be changed.

Alternatively, if consumers expect prices to rise in the future, they likely will accelerate buying today to beat the price rises. This reaction of course causes an increase in today's aggregate demand and causes prices to rise. This phenomenon is a major part of the hyperinflation process touched on in Chapter 1. As people expect higher prices, they accelerate buying which pushes up prices which makes people expect higher prices, which makes people accelerate their buying, and so on.

**Figure 4-4  Changes in Aggregate Supply and Impacts on Real GDP and Inflation**

More available economic resources
Cheaper economic resources
Higher productivity
More favorable government climate toward business
Higher business investment
More competition
        Lead to: increased aggregate supply
                Which leads to: higher real GDP
                            lower inflation

Less available economic resources
More expensive economic resources
Lower productivity
Less favorable government climate toward business
Lower business investment
Less competition
Currency collapse
        Lead to: lower aggregate supply
                Which leads to: lower real GDP
                            higher inflation

## Summary

1.  Trends in real GDP and inflation in the US, or any, economy, are caused by interaction of supply and demand actions by a variety

of economic actors — consumers, businesses, foreign economic entities, government entities, and central banks — in the economy's aggregate market for goods and services.

2. Recession occurs when aggregate demand or aggregate supply falls. Expansion occurs when aggregate demand or aggregate supply rises.

3. Inflation accelerates in response to increases in aggregate demand or decreases in aggregate supply, and decelerates in response to lower aggregate demand or increased aggregate supply.

4. Aggregate demand rises when economic events encourage increased spending on the country's production of goods and services. Examples of such shifts include lower interest rates, increased consumer and business confidence, and increased foreign demand. Reverse trends, such as higher taxes, lower aggregate demand.

5. Aggregate supply rises when business' profits, expected profits, or its ability to produce are enhanced by events such as lower business taxes, lower input costs, increased availability of inputs, and decreased government regulation. Opposite trends, such as higher input costs and reductions in productivity, as well as currency collapses, decrease aggregate supply.

# 5 | Causes of Unemployment and Interest Rate Trends

As with real GDP and inflation, the concepts of supply and demand and their interaction can be used to understand trends in unemployment and interest rates.

## Understanding Trends in Unemployment

Unemployment occurs as a result of imbalance between demand for labor (employment) and supply of labor (the labor force) in the labor market. To understand the causes of unemployment therefore requires understanding determinants of demand for and supply of labor.

### Demand for Labor

The demand for labor, in effect the number of workers business wishes to hire, is determined by four key factors.

- The overall level of economic activity — i.e. the level of real GDP — probably is the most important single determinant. When real GDP increases, the demand for labor rises as businesses hire more workers to produce the additional output, and unemployment falls as the increased jobs remove individuals from unemployment. The reverse is true for declines in real GDP. It is this relationship that explains why unemployment is high in recession.

- A second important factor is the wage rate. An important principle of business economics is that business will attempt to reduce its use of any input which has increased in price. Thus, if wage rates are rising, business will attempt to reduce its use of labor, which will reduce the demand for labor. To a great extent, it is this factor — i.e., high US wages relative to the the rest of the world — that is causing US businesses to establish factories in other countries. Lower wages will of course encourage the use of labor.

- A third factor is the skill and productivity of the labor force, with a more skilled / productive labor force creating a greater demand for labor and a less skilled / productive labor force creating lesser demand for labor.

- A fourth factor that affects the demand for labor is technological progress. While in the long-run, technological progress is thought to be beneficial, in the short-run it often reduces the demand for labor and jobs, especially lower-skill jobs, since much technological progress displaces jobs as it is implemented on the shop flow — robots instead of workers welding car parts together, for example. Figure 5-1 shows three categories into which economists group the various causes of unemployment.

### Figure 5-1 Types of Unemployment

- Frictional unemployment refers to unemployment that occurs as a result of the fact that labor markets do not work perfectly or instantly. In other words, even when plenty of jobs are available and plenty of qualified workers are available, it often takes some time for the two to get matched up. During this time, these people "between jobs" will be unemployed and considered as frictionally unemployed. As much of this unemployment is voluntary, economists and policymakers do not consider frictional unemployment as a substantial problem.

- Cyclical unemployment is that unemployment that is linked to the business cycle. It rises in recession and falls in expansion, and is associated with a worker being "laid off". Cyclical unemployment is considered to be more severe a problem because much of this unemployment is involuntary and, during recessions, the numbers of people cyclically unemployed can be very large. It is not considered the most severe type of unemployment, however, because cyclically unemployed have good prospects of returning to work when the recession ends and economic expansion returns.

- The most severe type of unemployment is structural unemployment. In this type of unemployment, the cause is a mismatch between the labor skills the economy needs and the labor skills workers have. When there is such a mismatch — i.e. many workers either have no skills or skills not needed by the economy — structural unemployment will rise. This type of unemployment is a major problem because structurally unemployed workers have little or no prospect of finding a job. Structural unemployment tends to be high when an economy is experiencing substantial structural change, as is occurring in the United States at present, or when the labor market contains significant barriers to flexibility, as is the case in Europe at present. Structural unemployment must be dealt with by removal of impediments and by workers being retrained into skills the economy needs.

## Supply of Labor

The supply for labor is determined largely by two main factors.

- One important factor is population growth, particularly of the prime working ages of 18-65. If this age group is growing rapidly, as occurred in the United States in the 1970s and 1980s because of the "Baby Boom Generation", then labor supply likely will also grow rapidly. Conversely, if the adult population grows slowly, as will be the US case for the next several years, labor force and labor supply growth will be slower. The rate of immigration into a country also affects the growth of population and labor supply.

- A second labor supply factor is what economists call the labor force participation rate, i.e., the rate at which individuals choose to participate in the working labor force, as opposed to not joining the labor force. Again, in the past 20 years, the United States has witnessed important trends in this area, notably the sharp increases in the participation rates of women. When the participation rate rises, the supply of labor rises, and when the participation rate falls, the supply of labor falls.

## The Role of Unions

A factor which works on both the demand for and supply of labor is the strength of unions. When unions are strong, they are able to hold down the supply of labor and bid up wages. While this action raises wages for those persons, often union members, who obtain jobs, the higher wage rates also reduces demand for labor and raises unemployment.

Putting these forces and their effects together yields the following conclusions. Unemployment will most likely rise when: the economy is in recession, wages have been raised inordinately high by unions, the adult population is growing rapidly, labor force participation rates are rising, and there is rapid change in the structure of the economy. Unemployment most likely will fall when opposite conditions are present.

Figure 5-2 shows how US unemployment has changed over the past two decades in the context of these factors. As the figure shows, unemployment rose in the 1970s and fell, albeit slightly, between 1987 and 1997. The most important cause of this difference was differences in labor supply growth. In the 1970s, for example, the US labor force grew by 24 million, whereas from 1987 to 1997 it expanded only 16 million.

## The Labor Market and Wages

Interactions between labor supply and labor demand affect not only unemployment, but also the price of labor, the wage rate. For example, another reason that US unemployment fell from 1987 to 1997 was that wages declined in real terms, making US labor less expensive to use and inducing businesses to hire more workers. In turn, one of the reasons for the decline in wages was rapid growth in labor supply relative to labor demand which, particularly in the context of weaker US unions, drove down wage rates.

Figure 5-2 United States: Changes in Unemployment and Determinants

|  | 1970-80 | 1987-97 |
|---|---|---|
| Change in Unemployment (millions) | 3.6 | -0.7 |
|  |  |  |
| Change in Labor Force (millions) | 24.2 | 16.4 |
| Change in Participation Rate (percentage points) | 1.7 | 1.5 |
| Change in Adult Population (millions) | 30.7 | 20.4 |
|  |  |  |
| Change in Employment (millions) | 20.7 | 17.1 |
| Change in Real GDP (percent) | 31.3 | 27.3 |
| Change in Real Wage Rates (percent) | -8.0 | -5.4 |

Source: Council of Economic Advisers, *Economic Report of the President, 1998.*

In contrast, in Europe, where unions have remained strong, wage rates continued to increase, but with the result of stagnant demand for labor and severe unemployment. Thus, depending on other characteristics of a country's labor market, drops in demand for labor or increases in supply of labor will sometimes cause more unemployment and will sometimes cause lower wages.

## Understanding Changes in Interest Rates

The other domestic performance measure examined in this chapter is interest rates, the price of borrowed or loaned money, determined by supply and demand forces in a country's capital markets.

In this capital market, demand for loanable funds generally comes from five groups:

- businesses who borrow money to invest to expand or upgrade their productive capacity;

- consumers who borrow to make "big-ticket" purchases such as cars, houses, and large appliances that they are unable to pay for out of current earnings;

- state and local governments, who borrow money on their capital budgets to make capital improvements such as roads, schools, prisons, etc.

- the Federal government, which borrows money whenever it runs a budget deficit, which has been every year since 1960 except one (again, more on this in Chapter 7);

- and foreign borrowers, who in today's global economy, can tap the US capital market as well as their own.

The supply of loanable funds generally comes from four main sources that in some cases overlap the users of loanable funds:

- households that in fact spend less, not more, than they earn, allowing them to generate savings which then are supplied to the country's capital market;

- businesses that generate a greater cash flow than they need and make it possible for them to supply funds to the capital market;

- foreign economic entities that, instead of obtaining money on the US capital market, choose to supply money to that market;

- and nations' central banks which often use their power to create new money to add funds to their countries' loanable funds market.

Obviously, within some of these groups, some elements are saving and lending and others are borrowing, and what is going on balance may be either saving or borrowing. In the case of the United States, at present, the picture is as follows: US households are net savers, albeit at a low rate, and suppliers of funds to US capital markets; US businesses are net borrowers; government entities, including state, local, and Federal, are net savers (i.e., budget surpluses); foreign economic entities are net suppliers of funds to the US capital market; and the Federal Reserve, the US central bank discussed in Chapter 8, is creating new money each year to add to the capital pool.

Interest rates are determined in this capital market by interactions between these supplies of and demands for these investment funds. When demand for funds is high or supply of funds is low, interest rates will be high; when the demand is low or the supply is high, interest rates will be low.

- Thus, high interest rates likely will be caused by: low household savings, high business investment and consumer spending, a large budget deficit, a low rate of new money creation by the central bank, or low net inflows of foreign capital. High interest rates tend to occur during economic expansions since business investment and consumer spending are likeliest to be high during expansion.

- Conversely, low interest rates will be caused by high household savings, low business investment and consumer spending, a small budget deficit, a high rate of new money creation by the central bank, or high net inflows of foreign capital. Low interest rates tend to occur during recessions, since business investment and consumer spending are likeliest to be low during recession.

Interest rates also are strongly affected by inflation and expected inflation. Specifically, if a lender expects inflation to be high, that fact itself will tend to raise nominal interest rates as the lender requires a higher nominal interest rate to cover his real losses due to inflation. For example, if you were a lender, you would not want to lend money at 6 percent for 5 years and have the inflation rate over those five years be 12 percent; so, you, and other lenders, will protect in inflationary times by building into interest rates a sufficient inflation premium.

Another factor important to interest rate determination is expectations. In particular, much of what governs long-term interest rates is not what is going now but what is expected to go on in the future, since it will be in the future that lenders realize most of their returns from their loans. Thus, interest rates may change due to the expectation of some change that would affect future interest rates, such as expectation of higher inflation or a lower budget deficit, even before the change actually occurs. Interest rates appear to have become much more sensitive to expected future changes than they used to be. Figure 5-3 summarizes impacts of various forces on interest rates.

**Figure 5-3 Determinants of Interest Rates**

| |
|---|
| Interest rates tend to be made higher by: <br>        a stronger economy <br>        higher inflation <br>        a tighter monetary policy <br>        less inflows of foreign capital <br>        a larger budget deficit <br><br>Interest rates tend to be made lower by: <br>        a weaker economy <br>        lower inflation <br>        a looser monetary policy <br>        more inflows of foreign capital <br>        a smaller budget deficit |

We can now use these factors to help us examine trends in US interest rates, for example to assess why US long-term interest rates were high in 1984 — the long-term government bond rate in that year was 12 percent — and were lower in 1997 when the same rate was under 7 percent.

- In 1984, both supply and demand factors in the loanable funds market were contributing to higher interest rates. The Federal budget deficit was high and rising; real GDP growth was high; the household saving rate was falling; inflation, while falling, had been high; and the Federal Reserve was running a tight monetary policy (see Figure 5-4). Only increased inflows of foreign capital were acting to hold down US interest rates.

- In contrast, in 1997, the trends in these determinants of US interest rates were much different. The budget deficit was smaller and falling; real GDP growth was lower; inflation was low and had been for several years; the Federal Reserve's monetary policy was not quite as tight; and inflows of foreign capital to US capital markets had accelerated.

**Figure 5-4 United States: Causes of Interest Rate Trends, 1984 and 1997**

|  | 1984 | 1997 |
|---|---|---|
| Interest Rates (long-term govt. bonds) | 12.4 | 6.6 |
|  |  |  |
| Real GDP Growth (percent) | 6.2 | 3.7 |
| Inflation Rate (percent) | 3.9 | 1.7 |
| Change in Money Supply (percent) | 6.0 | 8.1 |
| Net Capital Inflows (billions of dollars) | 99.0 | 166.0 |
| Budget Deficit (percent of GDP) | 5.0 | 0.3 |

Source: Council of Economic Advisers, *Economic Report of the President, 1998.*

## Summary

1. Unemployment, determined in the labor market, is driven by the balance of the demand for labor, generated by business needing labor for its production processes, and the supply of labor, driven by adult population growth and labor force participation trends.

2. Factors that reduce demand for labor and push up unemployment include recession, rapid technological change, inordinately high wage rates, with opposite trends raising labor demand and reducing unemployment.

3. Factors that increase labor supply and push up unemployment include rapid working-age population growth, increasing labor force participation rates, and increased rates of immigration. Opposite trends in these areas will tend to hold down unemployment.

4. Changes in labor demand and supply do not only affect unemployment, however. Often, wages are also impacted, with falling labor demand and rising labor supply lowering wages instead of raising unemployment.

5. Interest rates are determined in a country's financial markets by the balance of the supply and demand for loanable and investable funds.

6. When the demand for loanable funds is high — as occurs when the economy is expanding, government budget deficits are large, and inflation is high — interest rates will be higher.

7. Higher interest rates also occur when the supply of loanable funds is low — as occurs when the central bank is implementing a tight monetary policy, domestic saving rates are low, and there are few inflows of foreign funds. Reverse trends in supply of and demand for loanable funds produce low interest rates.

# 6 | The International Balance of Payments and Exchange Rates

In this chapter, we move from discussing determinants of a country's domestic economic performance — real GDP, inflation, unemployment, and interest rates — to assessing determinants of its international economic situation — trade balance, current balance, international capital flows, international reserve position, and exchange rates. Determinants of balance of payments trends will be discussed first, followed by discussion of exchange rates. However, since balance of payments and exchange rate trends are jointly determined in foreign exchange and international financial markets, it would have been just as correct to begin the discussion with an examination of exchange rate determination.

## Determinants of Balance of Payments Flows

A country's balance of payment flows — the exports, imports, and capital flows discussed in Chapter 2 — are caused by a combination of domestic and foreign economic trends.

### Determinants of Exports, Imports, and Current Account Balances

Several factors determine a country's exports of goods and services.

- One key factor is the level of foreign economic activity. If foreign economies are doing well, they will be demanding higher levels of imported products, and raising demand for other countries' exports of goods and services. For example, US exports to Europe will be higher when Europe is in economic expansion than when Europe is in economic recession.

- Another key factor is the relation between a country's inflation rate and the inflation rate in other countries. When domestic inflation is high relative to foreign inflation, a country's products will be losing price competitiveness relative to foreign goods and, in turn, demand for its exports will fall. As a result, most countries that experience high inflation will also be seeing slow growth in exports.

- A third factor is how domestic productive capabilities are doing relative to foreign capabilities. If these domestic productive capabilities are doing well — i.e., are rising, are producing better products, are producing products with increased efficiency — then the result will be to shift world demand in the country's direction, and to lead to higher demand for its exports. One of the main reasons China is presently experiencing an export boom is this factor.

- A fourth factor is the exchange rate for the country's currency. When a country's currency exchange rate is appreciated, also often referred to as high, strong, or overvalued, the appreciated exchange rate will raise the cost, in their currencies, of foreigners buying the country's products. As a result, a high exchange rate will tend to reduce a country's exports.

Opposite trends in those factors will have opposite impacts on exports.

Determinants of a country's imports of goods and services are similar to export determinants.

- One factor is the level of domestic economic activity. If a country's domestic economy is in economic expansion, then it will be demanding higher level of imported products, and raising its imports of goods and services. US imports from Europe will be higher when the United States is in economic expansion than when it is in economic recession.

- Another factor is, again, the relation between a country's inflation rate and the inflation rate in other countries. For imports, the relationship is reverse that for exports. Specifically, when domestic inflation is high relative to foreign inflation, a country's products will be losing price competitiveness relative to foreign goods and, in turn, its imports will rise as domestic consumers and businesses turn to the cheaper foreign products for their purchases.

- How well basic domestic productive capabilities are doing relative to foreign capabilities also affects a country's imports as well as its exports. If these domestic production capabilities are doing well — i.e., are rising, are producing better products, are producing products with increased efficiency — then the result will be to shift a country's own demand inward, and to reduce demand for imports.

- As with exports, a country's exchange rate is extremely important in determining the country's imports, but with an opposite effect. In the case of imports, an appreciated/strong/high/over-valued currency makes purchases of foreign products cheaper and causes a country's imports to rise.

- Finally, how open a country's market is to imports will affect the level of imports. If the market is closed — through government policy or corporate or cultural actions — imports will be less than they would be if the market was more open.

Opposite movements in these determinants will have opposite effects on imports and supplies of the country's currency on foreign exchange markets. Also, as discussed above, several determinants — inflation, production capabilities, and exchange rates — affect both exports and imports and do so in opposite directions. Figure 6-1 summarizes the determinants and their effects.

### Determinants of Capital Inflows and Outflows

A country's international capital inflows and outflows also are determined by underlying factors. These determinants are broadly related to investment returns and risk in the country when compared with investment returns and risk elsewhere. Specifically, when investment returns in the country are high relative to foreign investment returns and risks are low, and investment capital has mobility across national borders, as is the case in today's world (see Chapter 12), then the country is likely to experience higher capital inflows as foreign investors put their money in the higher return rates in the country and lower capital outflows as domestic investors keep their money in the country to take advantage of the higher relative returns. Conversely, if foreign investment returns are higher or risks lower, then lower capital inflows and higher capital outflows will result.

**Figure 6-1  Summary of Determinants of Exports and Imports**

Exports will rise (fall) and current balance will move toward surplus (deficit) when:

Foreign economic activity is strong (weak)
Domestic inflation is low (high)
Domestic competitiveness is high (low)
Exchange rate is depreciated (appreciated)

Imports will rise (fall) and current balance will move toward deficit (surplus) when:

Domestic economic activity is strong (weak)
Domestic inflation is high (low)
Domestic competitiveness is low (high)
Exchange rate is appreciated (depreciated)
The domestic market is more (less) open to imports

Specific relationships likely to affect these relative returns and in turn determine capital inflows and outflows include the following.

- If domestic interest rates are high relative to foreign rates, capital inflows will rise and capital outflows will fall. One reason the United States experienced net capital inflows in the 1980s — also called a capital account surplus — was high US interest rates.

- If returns on a country's business operations — i.e., profits — are high relative to foreign returns, capital inflows will be higher and capital outflows will be lower. Because of the strong US economy, a weak European economy, and favorable tax treatment of returns on business operations, the United States has experienced strong net capital inflows in the 1990s.

- If the domestic political economic environment is perceived as less risky relative to foreign environments, then capital inflows will increase and capital outflows will decrease. This relationship has been illustrated in Russia in the 1990s, but in a reverse manner. Specifically, because of the immense instability and uncertainty in that country, Russia has experienced massive net capital outflows, called capital flight, leading to a huge capital account deficit — with some estimates ranging as high as $20 billion a year.

Opposite situations for these relationships will produce opposite trends in capital inflows and outflows.

Finally, as with current account flows, the exchange rate itself impacts on international capital flows of a country, but the impacts are more complex than for current account flows. On the one hand, when the exchange rate is appreciated, capital inflows are reduced due to the expense added to investing in the country by the higher exchange rate, and capital outflows are raised as the higher exchange rate reduces the costs of foreign investments. A depreciated exchange rate obviously has opposite effects.

However, if an appreciation or depreciation of an exchange rate creates expectations of further appreciation or depreciation, then the impacts on international capital flows can be reversed. For example, if a currency's depreciation causes investors to expect further depreciation, then the depreciation will cause more, not fewer, capital outflows. This expectational factor plays an important role in currency collapses. Figure 6-2 summarizes the determinants of a country's capital inflows and outflows.

**Figure 6-2 Summary of Determinants of International Capital Flows**

Capital Inflows Will Rise, Capital Outflows Will Fall, and a Capital Account Surplus (Net Capital Inflows) Will Result When:

domestic interest rates rise relative to foreign interest rates
domestic profits rise relative to foreign profits
domestic stability is high relative to foreign stability
the exchange rate is depreciated
the exchange is expected to appreciate

Opposite trends will produce decreases in capital inflows, increases in capital outflows, and a capital account deficit (Net Capital Outflows).

## Interactions among Balance of Payments, Exchange Rates, and Reserves

The previous section noted that exchange rates and their movements affected balance of payment flows but did not discuss what caused exchange rates to settle at certain levels or change in the first place. This section addresses the way in which balance of payments flows impact on exchange rates in floating exchange systems and on official international reserves in fixed exchange rate situations.

Overall surpluses in a country's balance of payments — created by increases in exports and capital inflows or decreases in imports and capital outflows — cause an excess demand for the country's currency on foreign exchange markets. Conversely, overall deficits in a country's balance of payments — created by decreases in exports and capital inflows or increases in imports or capital outflows — cause an excess supply of the country's currency on foreign exchange markets.

In a floating exchange rate system — the system in which the exchange rate is allowed to adjust to imbalances in the balance of payments — the surplus situation will cause the exchange rate to appreciate and the deficit situation will cause the exchange rate to depreciate. (Remember, however, these outcomes apply only to an overall surplus or deficit and imbalances individual sub-accounts do not always indicate overall imbalance.) In turn, the changes in the exchange rate will create forces that will eliminate the surplus or deficit. If the initial situation is one of surplus, the exchange rate will appreciate. This appreciation will cause a drop in exports and capital inflows by making them more expensive, will cause a rise in imports and capital outflows by making them less expensive, and together these two responses will eliminate the surplus. A reverse process would eliminate a deficit.

In a fixed exchange rate system, however, a different outcome will occur. Through actions to be discussed in detail in Chapter 8, the central bank will absorb the surplus or deficit that would otherwise cause the exchange rate to appreciate or depreciate. In doing so, it will prevent the exchange rate from moving, but its actions also will cause changes in its holdings of international reserves — a rise in reserves in an underlying surplus situation and a fall in reserves in a deficit situation. Figure 6-3 summarizes the inter-relationships among balance of payment flows and exchange rates.

**Figure 6-3**
**Summary of Interactions between Balance of Payments and Exchange Rates**

Higher exports of goods and services
Higher inward transfers
Higher capital inflows
Lower imports of goods and services
Lower outward transfers
Lower capital outflows

Will cause: A tendency toward a balance of payments surplus

Which will cause

In a floating exchange rate system, exchange rate appreciation which will return the prospective balance of payments surplus to balance by lowering exports and capital inflows and raising imports and capital outflows.

In a fixed exchange rate system, central bank intervention to prevent exchange rate appreciation, which will allow the balance of payments surplus to occur and cause the country to gain international reserves.

Lower exports of goods and services
Lower inward transfers
Lower capital inflows
Higher imports of goods and services
Higher outward transfers
Higher capital outflows.

Will cause: A tendency toward a balance of payments deficit

Which will cause:

In a floating exchange rate system, exchange rate depreciation which will return the prospective balance of payments surplus to balance by raising exports and capital inflows and lowering imports and capital outflows.

In a fixed exchange rate system, central bank intervention to prevent exchange rate depreciation which will allow the balance of payments deficit to occur and cause the country to lose international reserves.

Figure 6-4 provides a graphical representation of how balance of payments flows and exchange rate interactions can be examined in the graphical supply and demand framework used to understand real GDP changes and inflation in Chapter 4. In this graph, the vertical axis shows a currency's exchange rate, with an increase representing an appreciation and a decrease representing a depreciation. The demand line in this graph represents balance of payments flows associated with the credit side of the balance of payments — exports, capital inflows, and transfers in — as these flows require demanding of the nation's currency on foreign exchange markets to make these transactions. The supply line represents balance of payments flows associated with the debit side of the balance of payments — imports, capital outflows, and transfers out — as these flows require supplying of the nation's currency on foreign exchange markets.

**Figure 6-4**
**Supply and Demand Analysis of Balance of Payments and Exchange Rates**

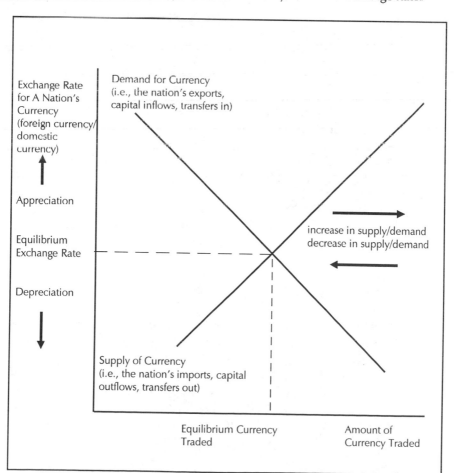

As with other supply and demand graphs, this graph allows an analysis of the impacts on exchange rates of various economics events by shifting the supply or demand lines to the right or left as the events increase or decrease the various balance of payment flows. For example, a sudden rise in a nation's competitiveness would — according to Figure 6-3 — cause a rise in its exports and a decline in its imports. In the graph, this outcome would cause a leftward shift in the supply line, a rightward shift in the demand line, and upward pressure on the exchange rate. Or, a fall in domestic investment returns or rise in investment risk would cause capital outflows to increase and inflows to decrease, shifting the supply line to the right, the demand line to the left, and placing downward pressure on the exchange rate. In turn, the exchange rate changes causes movement along the new supply and demand lines until a new equilibrium exchange rate is reached.

As can be seen from examination of Figures 6-3 and 6-4, a floating exchange rate system has a tendency to automatically adjust itself to shifts that would move balance of payments out of balance. For example, assume that a country's exports of goods and services increase. This event would lead to an initial balance of payments surplus followed by appreciation of the country's exchange rate which would in turn lead to a fall in exports and capital inflows, rise in imports and capital outflows, and return the balance of payments toward balance.

Or, suppose that massive outflows of capital occurred from a country. This event would create a balance of payments deficit which in turn would cause a major depreciation of the currency which in turn would boost exports and capital inflows, reverse or at least slow the capital outflows, reduce imports, and move the deficit back toward a surplus.

In a fixed rate system, since the exchange rate does not adjust, this balancing process will not occur. Instead, in the two examples given above, the country will actually experience a surplus and its central bank accumulate international reserves (first example) or actually experience a deficit and its central bank lose international reserves (second example).

## Real World Examples

As an example of how balance of payments and exchange rates and reserves interact, suppose a country with a floating exchange rate initially was in current account balance, capital account balance, and, therefore, in overall balance. Then suppose that domestic interest rates rise. In this situation, the higher interest rates will cause a capital account surplus (capital inflows up, capital outflows down). In turn the capital account surplus will cause the exchange rate to appreciate, reducing somewhat the tendency of the capital account to go into surplus, but also pushing the current account into deficit as the appreciating exchange rate reduces exports and boosts imports.

After all is said and done, the higher domestic interest rates lead to: higher capital inflows, lower capital outflows, and a capital account surplus; an appreciation of the exchange rate; higher imports of goods and services, lower exports of goods and services, and a current account deficit; and a return to overall non-official balance of payments equilibrium. This example typifies exactly what happened in the United States in the mid 1980s, when high domestic interest rates caused large capital inflows, an appreciated currency, and a substantial trade and current account deficit.

If, however, the exchange rate is fixed, the outcome is different. In the example above, for instance, the exchange rate would not have been allowed to appreciate, and the country would have stayed in overall non-official balance of payments surplus and steadily gained official international reserves. This latter outcome is largely what happened to Germany in late 1992, when its interest rates soared, caused massive inflows of capital from the rest of Europe, and led to a large German capital and overall balance of payments surplus. Because Germany's exchange rate was fixed, the surplus actually occurred and dramatically increased Germany's official reserves.

Following are four additional real world examples of how economic trends and policies, balance of payments flows, and exchange rates interact.

- Through most of the 1980s and 1990s, South Korea was gaining competitiveness rapidly, resulting in sharp increases in demands for its exports and an increasing current account surplus. This outcome should have caused the exchange rate for South Korea's currency to have appreciated, but in order to enhance their competitiveness, the South Korean central bank fixed their exchange at an arbitrarily low level. As a result, South Korea ran an overall balance of payments surplus and accumulated large additions to its official international reserves.

- In an opposite example, throughout most the late 1980s, India arbitrarily fixed its exchange rate at an inordinately high level. As a result of this action, India ran large deficits in both its current account, due to Indian goods being too expensive on world markets, and its capital account, due to the overvalued exchange rate making it too expensive for foreign investors to want to invest in India. However, the actions India's central bank had to take to absorb the excessive supplies of its currency on international financial markets — i.e., the overall balance of payments deficit — meant steady and sometimes dramatic losses in its international reserves, such that by 1991, India was virtually out of reserves.

- In 1993, Mexico experienced a rise in official reserves (overall balance of payments surplus) as large capital inflows to invest in Mexico's newly-reformed economy more than offset a current account deficit. However, a political crisis in 1994 reversed the capital flows and created, along with the current account deficit, an overall deficit. Initially, Mexico tried to keep the exchange rate fixed but used up so many reserves it experienced a financial crisis and had to let the exchange rate depreciate.

- Most recently, a rise in the perceived risk of East Asian investments led to large withdrawals of portfolio capital (bank deposits, loans, mutual funds). These withdrawals put downward pressure on these countries' currencies, which they first defended with their international reserves, but then, when reserves were depleted, had to let their currencies fall dramatically.

## Summary

1.  The determination of a country's balance of payments trends and its exchange rate movements occurs through workings of market forces in the market for international finance and foreign exchange.

2.  In this market, a country's exports, inward transfers, and capital inflows create demand for the country's currency, and its imports, outward transfers, and capital outflows create supplies of the country's currency.

3.  These demands for and supplies of a currency on international financial markets are determined by a variety of forces.

4.  Trends such as higher domestic incomes, more competitive foreign products, higher foreign investment returns, domestic instability, and an overvalued exchange rate push the balance of payments toward deficit by increasing imports of goods and services and/or capital outflows.

5.  Opposite trends in incomes, competitiveness, investment returns, stability, and the exchange rate will produce a movement of a country's balance of payments toward surplus.

6.  In a floating exchange system, a tendency toward deficit or surplus in a country's overall non-official balance of payments will cause the exchange rate to depreciate or appreciate, respectively, which will return the balance of payments back to balance, although with changed values of the various balance of payments flows.

7. In a fixed exchange rate system, in contrast, the fixed exchange rate will cause the deficit or surplus to actually occur and the country's central bank to lose official international reserves in a deficit situation and gain reserves in a surplus situation.

8. In today's world, capital flows and investor perceptions are the most important determinants of exchange rate and balance of payment movements.

# 7 | Fiscal Policy, Budget Deficits, and the National Debt

This chapter marks a turn from examining the basic private sector forces which determine nations' economic performances to examination of ways the government tries to affect these performances. In doing so, it addresses some economic issues about which we hear a great deal — fiscal policy, the budget deficit and the national debt. All three are aspects of national governments' attempts to manage trends in a nation's economy — especially real GDP and inflation.

These attempts had their beginnings in the 1930s. Previously, the prevailing wisdom was that the economy would manage itself — i.e. normal forces would prevent recessions, inflation, or unemployment from "getting out of hand." However, the Great Depression, referred to in Chapter 1, changed that thinking. Out of that experience of 30 percent drops in real GDP and 25 percent unemployment came a re-looking at the role of government in managing overall economic trends.

The most influential of this re-looking was a book by an Englishman named John Maynard Keynes that provided a theoretical basis for active government intervention in the economy — a new set of economic principles and policy recommendations that even many non-economists know as Keynesianism. Although the belief in the ability of fiscal policy to solve problems of recession, unemployment, and inflation is much less strong today than it was at the height of Keynesianism in the 1960s, almost every national government still practices it to some extent.

## An Overview of The Tools of Fiscal Policy

Fiscal policy is essentially the national government changing tax rates and government spending with the intent of having some overall macroeconomic effect, usually either combatting recession or inflation. Before getting into the specific ways in which fiscal policy is applied, however, it will be useful to overview the tools of fiscal policy — tax rates and government spending.

## Taxation

Taxation, as most of us know, is the action of the government requiring private sector citizens and businesses to give the government money based on certain criteria.

- One major tax is the income tax. This tax assesses taxes on the basis of individuals' incomes, less whatever deductions, exemptions, credits, loopholes, etc. the tax code allows for. Many countries, including the United States, also levy taxes on the incomes of corporate businesses.

- Another major tax is the social security tax. This tax is levied on both earnings received by workers and payrolls paid by employers.

- The sales tax — levied exclusively by state and local governments in the United States, although also by national governments in Europe in the form of the value added tax (VAT) — is another important tax. This tax, rather than being levied on income, is levied on consumption.

Other taxes include import tariffs, inheritance and estate taxes, and excise taxes — sales taxes levied on the sales of specific items, like liquor, tobacco products, and telephone usage. Figure 7-1 presents the relative importance of various US taxes.

In terms of understanding the impact of taxes on economic activity, three main principles should be kept in mind. One principle is that who the tax is directly levied on is not always who pays the tax, or in economists' terminology, "bears the burden of the tax." Any economic entity that is taxed will try to "pass the tax on." This action is most often and directly done by businesses who raise prices paid by consumers, and is seen most when you make a retail purchase and the merchant adds the percent of the tax directly onto the cost of the purchase to acquire the funds which it must remit to the taxing authority for the tax. Other, less obvious, shifting also goes on. For example, if you rent an apartment, you do not pay property taxes directly, but you can count on some of the tax that your landlord pays being incorporated into your rental charges.

A second principle is that taxation of an economic activity discourages that activity from being carried out. Sometimes this principle is consciously applied, as when imports are taxed to reduce them or when so-called "sin" taxes are levied on alcohol and tobacco to discourage their use. However, this principle is always in operation and therefore creates economic disincentives even when not desired. For example, taxation of income to obtain revenue may obtain revenue, but it also will discourage income-creating activities, i.e., work and entrepreneurship, especially if the tax rate is high. Or, often the main result of a local government trying to obtain revenue from a sales tax will be simply to drive all retail activity to an adjacent jurisdiction with a lower sales tax.

Figure 7-1   US Tax Rates

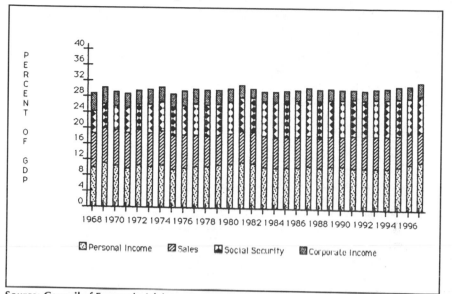

Source: Council of Economic Advisers, *Economic Report of the President, 1998.*

At the national level, this principle was used in reverse during President Ronald Reagan's first term in what came to be known as supply-side economics. In that term, President Reagan obtained a large tax cut designed, according to his campaign promises, to "Put America Back to Work!". In effect, his program believed that a cut in taxes on income would cause a greater amount of income-creating activities. Indeed, some of his advisers claimed that the income-creating response would be so great that tax revenues would be higher after the tax cut than before. That extreme claim did not come to pass, but the tax cut did lead to substantially more economic activity, as this principle suggests would be the case.

The third principle, and the one primarily utilized by fiscal policy, is that higher taxes lead to reduced after-tax income and, in turn, to reduced spending. This reduced spending drops aggregate demand and spurs decreases in real GDP and inflation, as discussed in Chapter 4. Decreases in taxes will increase aggregate demand, real GDP, and inflation. Figure 7-2 summarizes the impacts of changes in tax rates.

## Government Spending

The other tool commonly applied in fiscal policy is changes in government spending. While many types of government spending are carried out, economists usually group spending into two broad groups. The first group is purchases of economic goods and services by some government entity — i.e., the spending of government funds that is directly associated with some private economic actor providing a good or service in return. Examples of government purchases of goods and services include the Federal government paying a defense contractor to build an aircraft carrier, a state government paying a construction company to build a highway, and a local government paying administrators and teachers to provide educational services.

### Figure 7-2 Impacts of Changes in Tax Rates

Higher Tax Rates:
Increase government revenue (usually)
Reduce private sector disposable incomes and spending
Reduce aggregate demand
Reduce incentive to do taxed activity

Lower Tax Rates:
Decrease government revenue (usually)
Raise private sector disposable incomes and spending
Increase aggregate demand
Increase incentive to do activity on which taxes lowered

The other broad category of spending into which economists group outlays by governments is called transfer payments. It is spending which provides government funds to individuals or businesses not in payment for a economic good or service provided but because the political process deems the individuals or businesses needy or worthy of the transfer payment. Many categories of transfer payments are very familiar, such as social security payments, welfare payments, and Medicare and Medicaid payments, but other transfer payments also exist, such as agricultural support payments.

A final major group of government spending is the interest payments the government must make on its outstanding debt (see the "National Debt" section later in this chapter). As Figure 7-3 shows, government spending going to transfer payments and interest payments has risen dramatically over the past two decades.

Like taxation, government spending has a number of economic impacts.

- First, it affects spending and aggregate demand, and, through the process described in Chapter 3, real GDP and inflation. Increases in government spending will cause higher aggregate demand, real GDP, and inflation, and lower government spending will cause lower aggregate demand, real GDP, and inflation. These principles apply to changes in both government purchases and transfer payments.

- Second, it stimulates more of the action toward which the spending is directed. For the most part, this reaction is sensible and desired — i.e., if the Federal government spends more money on aircraft carriers, hopefully more aircraft carriers will be built. However, particularly in the area of transfer payments, this principle often produces perverse effects. For example, if the government pays medical bills, more people likely will demand medical services; if the government provides more generous unemployment benefits, more people may be content not to work; and if the government provides more generous agricultural support payments, excessive farm products will be produced.

**Figure 7-3  US Government Spending Trends**

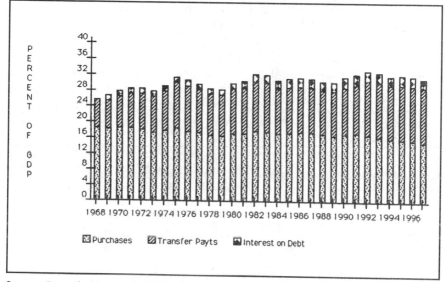

Source: Council of Economic Advisers, *Economic Report of the President, 1998.*

## Fiscal Policy in Action

Fiscal policy is implemented when the government — almost always the central or Federal government — alters tax rates, government purchases, or transfer payments with the explicit objective of changing aggregate demand and in turn real GDP or inflation. Fiscal policy takes two directions. Expansionary fiscal policy is shifts in tax rates and/or spending in a way to increase aggregate demand. Contractionary fiscal policy is shifts in tax rates and/or spending in a way to decrease aggregate demand. Expansionary fiscal policy most often is undertaken during recession, and contractionary fiscal policy most often is undertaken when the economy is experiencing too much inflation.

Given an expansionary fiscal policy is intended to increase aggregate demand, its key elements are cuts in tax rates or increases in government spending. The cuts in tax rates produce higher aggregate demand by leaving more income in the hands of consumers and businesses which for the most part they use to increase spending. The increases in transfer payments have a similar effect by putting more unemployment compensation, welfare payments, or other type of transfer payments into consumers' hands which they for the most part spend. Finally, increased government purchases of goods and services directly boost aggregate demand.

According to the principles of Chapter 4, each method will produce the desired result of raising real GDP out of recession as the higher aggregate demand boosts real GDP. However, an expansionary fiscal policy will also produce two undesirable side effects. By boosting aggregate demand, it also will put greater inflationary pressure in the economy, and, by raising spending and/or lowering taxes, it will create or increase the government budget deficit; more on the latter effect later in this chapter. Expansionary fiscal policy has occurred in the United States numerous times — which is one of the reasons the Federal Government ran regular budget deficits until 1998. One specific example occurred in 1975, when in response to the recession going on in that year, the Federal Government cut everyone's income taxes.

Contractionary fiscal policy produces opposite results — lower aggregate demand, lower inflation (the desired result), and a lower budget deficit, but also lower real GDP. In other words, one of the possible prices of combatting inflation with a contractionary fiscal policy is a recession. However, some economists believe that the reduced budget deficit will partly or wholly offset the recessionary impacts of a contractionary fiscal policy by lowering interest rates and stimulating economic activity (see below).

## Budget Deficits and Their Impacts

As discussed in the previous section, a major offshoot of an expansionary fiscal policy is creating or enlarging a government budget deficit, an outcome that occurs when government spending exceeds government tax and other revenues. However, in addition to being the result of fiscal policy, the budget balance also is influenced by the state of the economy. In particular, the budget tends to be more in deficit during recession because of drops in tax collections and increases in transfer payments like unemployment compensation. For the United States, the Federal government budget has largely been in deficit since 1960 (see Figure 7-4), an outcome that was typical of many other countries also. However, many governments dramatically reduced deficits in the mid 1990s, including the United States (see Figure 7-5).

When the US or other Government runs a budget deficit, it does not print money, as much commentary often asserts. The money creation process belongs to the central bank, like the Federal Reserve System, and will be discussed in Chapter 8. That said, much does happen in response to a government budget deficit. In effect, a budget deficit causes the

Federal Government to become a borrower of funds on financial markets. It does so by selling financial instruments called treasury bills, notes, and bonds; the familiar US savings bonds are, for example, one way the US Government obtains money to cover the deficit. This borrowing occurs in the same domestic financial markets described in Chapter 5, with the budget deficit adding to the demand for loanable funds in that market. Purchasers of treasury notes, bills, and bonds include individuals, businesses, banks, foreign investors, and, as will be discussed more in Chapter 8, the country's central bank.

**Figure 7-4  US Budget Deficit Trends**

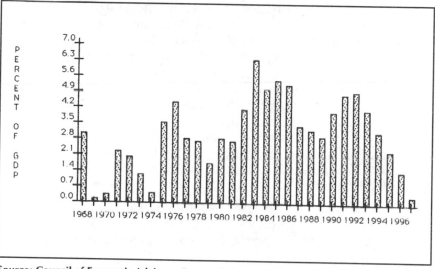

Source: Council of Economic Advisers, *Economic Report of the President, 1998.*

The increase in demand for loanable funds that is associated with a government budget deficit causes one impact of a budget deficit to be upward pressures on interest rates. In turn, the higher interest rates can discourage private investment, an effect that is often called "crowding out", an illusion to the effect of increased government borrowing crowding out private borrowing and investment.

Figure 7-5  Budget Balance of United States and Selected Other Countries, 1997 (percent of GDP)

| | |
|---|---|
| United States | -0.3 |
| Italy | -1.6 |
| Germany | -2.1 |
| Mexico | -1.3 |
| Sweden | -1.0 |

Source: International Monetary Fund, *International Financial Statistics*, August 1998.

Of course, while higher budget deficits will put upward pressure on interest rates, they do not always cause higher interest rates, since other determinants of interest rates may offset the impact of the deficits. For example, even though the US Federal budget deficit was still very large in the early 1990s, interest rates had fallen to quite low levels because the recession had dramatically lowered borrowing by private businesses and households.

## National Debt

Another concept related to fiscal policy is the national debt. Actually the term is somewhat of a misnomer, since it is not the debt of the nation, but rather the total outstanding debt of the Federal government. Some countries use the more accurate term of the public debt.

In effect, this national or public debt is the total of all the budget deficits the government has ever run, less any surpluses. Since there have been few surpluses, and no large surpluses, what we have is a large national debt, again an outcome matched by many other countries. At the end of 1997, for example, the US national debt stood at over $5 trillion, but, as always, care must be used in using nominal values which are affected by inflation. As with the budget deficit and other measures, a better way to portray the national debt is as a share of GDP (see Figure 7-6).

The national debt has a number of important economic implications.

- The national debt forces the Federal Government to allocate revenues to the paying of interest on the debt. In 1996, for example, over $240 billion, or 15 percent, of Federal spending went to pay this interest.

**Figure 7-6  US National Debt**

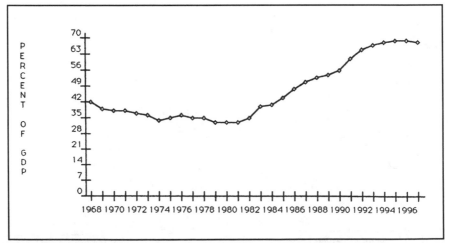

**Source: Council of Economic Advisers, *Economic Report of the President, 1997.***

- Since the national debt is held mostly by the wealthy, taxing to pay interest on the debt results in a redistribution of income away from lower and middle income taxpayers to wealthy holders of the national debt.

- If a lot of the national debt is held by foreigners, the interest paid on the national debt actually leaves the country. This factor is not a major problem in the United States — only about 15 percent of the US national debt is foreign-held — but has caused major problems for other countries.

## Interaction of Fiscal Policy with International Economic Trends

In today's world of internationalized economies, fiscal policy also has major interactions with a country's international economic performances.

- Expansionary fiscal policy often boosts imports and pushes the current account toward deficit, while contractionary fiscal policy slows imports and pushes it toward surplus.

- The higher interest rates that frequently result from budget deficits lead to increases in net inflows of foreign capital seeking higher domestic interest rates.

In today's world of integrated financial markets, it appears that the impact of a budget deficit on capital flows outweighs impacts on trade flows. Consequently, a budget deficit generally is thought to push a country's balance of payments into surplus if the exchange rate is fixed or causes the exchange rate to appreciate if the exchange rate is floating, with the appreciation in turn often causing the trade and current account to go into deficit.

An example of a budget deficit causing a balance of payments surplus and gains in reserves in a fixed exchange rate situation was Germany after it used deficit financing to pay the costs of its re-unification in 1991; an example of a budget deficit leading to exchange rate appreciation in a floating exchange rate situation was the United States in the early 1980s.

This impact of budget deficits on international capital flows, made possible by the increased globalization of investment capital flows, has implications for domestic impacts of fiscal policy. In particular, the capital inflows drawn by the higher interest rates means that a government can draw on capital from the rest of the world to finance its deficits, an outcome which mitigates the rise in interest rates and makes it easier for the country to finance its deficits, but which also can cause considerable tension among the countries who are losing capital to finance another country's budget deficit. Britain, for example, was disturbed at the

German budget deficit in 1992 causing outflows of British capital to finance that deficit.

## Expectations and Lags

Changes in fiscal policy also have impacts on expectations, and, through them, on economic decisions and performance. One of the most important of these exceptional impacts is thought by some economists to be with regard to the budget deficit. Specifically, many economists believe that larger budget deficits associated with expansionary fiscal policy have significant negative impacts on current economic performance as potential investors curtail investment because they expect deficits to cause future higher interest rates or tax increases.

However, while logically correct — i.e., if you as an investor expected higher interest rates or taxes in the future, you might curtail your planned investments — the actual data on these expectational impacts is mixed. Early in the Bill Clinton Presidency, the relationship seemed to work, when a plan to cut the deficit was associated with increased economic activity. On the other hand, expectations of higher deficits were not associated with a slowdown in economic activity during President Ronald Reagan's first term. Of course, in both time periods, many other economic forces were at work, making it, as always in economics, difficult to disentangle the exact causes of a particular pattern of economic performance.

Another area in which many economists express concern regarding the usefulness of fiscal policy is related to the lag, or delays, in the impact of the policy. These economists believe that three specific lags create substantial problems for the implementation of fiscal policy. The first lag is called the recognition lag. By this, economists mean that because data on economic performance often is available only 2-3 months after the actual performance, there is a lag before an economic problem is recognized. The second lag is the decision lag — i.e., a delay in deciding the nature of the fiscal policy initiative. In our political system, because fiscal policy has to be an agreed response of the President and the Congress, this lag can be quite a long one. The final lag is the impact lag and relates to even after the new policy has been put in place, the full impacts may take several months to occur. Put together, these lags can often mean that it may be more than a year, sometimes longer, before a fiscal policy initiative actually impacts, by which time the need for it may have passed.

# Summary

1. Fiscal policy involves changes in government tax rates or spending, almost always at the Federal level, to try to counter adverse overall trends in an economy, such as a recession or too much inflation.

2. An expansionary fiscal policy, generally undertaken during times of economic recession, involves cutting tax rates and/or increasing spending. While these actions, by boosting aggregate demand, usually have the desired result of raising real GDP, they also create negative side effects, notably larger budget deficits and greater inflationary pressures.

3. A contractionary fiscal policy, recommended for times of excessive inflation or too large budget deficits, produces opposite results — lower inflation, a lower budget deficit, but a greater risk of an economic slowdown or recession.

4. While fiscal policy focuses on the impacts on aggregate demand of changes in tax rates, tax rate changes also have impacts on aggregate supply. It is these impacts that so-called supply-side economics emphasize, calling for a reduction in tax rates, particularly on income earned from productive activities, to encourage more work, investment, and entrepreneurship to increase aggregate supply.

5. When government spending consistently outstrips government revenues, whether for fiscal policy or other reasons — until recently, a regular outcome in the United States, and most other countries for that matter — the outcome is perpetual budget deficits and steady increases in the so-called national debt.

6. While, if kept in bounds, budget deficits and a large national debt do not spell calamity for an economy — else the United States could not have done it for so long — continued deficits and increases in the national debt do create negative impacts on the economy — higher interest rates, less private investment, higher taxes to pay the interest on the debt, and, if the debt is held by foreigners, a loss in domestic income.

7. Some economists also believe that ongoing budget deficits and a large national debt also have indirect, but important, negative impacts on the economy through causing investors not to invest out of fear of future higher taxes or inflation as a result of the deficits and debt. Some economists also believe lags in the impact of a fiscal policy may undercut the usefulness of fiscal policy.

8.  In today's globally-linked economic system, changes in fiscal policy also affect a country's international economic trends. In particular, expansionary fiscal policy and higher budget deficits will, through impacts on interest rates and imports, create capital account surpluses and current account deficits, sometimes with impacts on the exchange rate if one impact is particularly stronger than the other.

9.  Because of reactions of international capital flows to budget deficits in today's world, fiscal policy can be more flexible, because it will cause shifts in international capital flows that will reinforce its intent. For example, an expansionary fiscal policy and its associated budget deficit will, through the resulting higher interest rates, attract funds from abroad that will help finance the deficit and hold down interest rates, making it more possible for a government to run deficits.

# 8 | The Federal Reserve System and Monetary Policy

In addition to fiscal policy, governmental authorities of most countries try to manage their country's overall economic trends through influencing conditions in the country's financial markets, particularly interest rates and the supplies of money and credit. These actions are generally carried out by an institution called the central bank, which is given authority over the nation's money supply. In the United States, the central bank is called the Federal Reserve System. This chapter examines the relationships among a country's macroeconomic performance, interest rates, money supply, and the actions of the central bank. It begins with a look at what money is and how it influences economic activity.

## Money

Money is that commodity whose primary use is to purchase other products or to store financial value to make those purchases later. In the United States, it is defined into a variety of successively more encompassing definitions according to the spendability of the financial items included. In its most narrow definition — the M1 definition of the money supply often referred to in newspapers — money includes coin, currency, and demand deposits, i.e. checking accounts. Successively broader definitions add to this narrow definition additional types of financial instruments. M2, for example, adds to M1 savings and small time deposits and some money market fund balances. M3 includes all that is in M2 plus large time deposits and additional money market fund balances. Figure 8-1 shows trends in the United States money supply.

As Figure 8-1 shows, one of the trends that has occurred over the years has been a progressive drop in importance of M1. Twenty years ago, most reference to monetary policy and the money supply used M1 as the primary definition. However, changes that have occurred in financial markets, such as creation of money market funds on which you can write checks and telephone transfer from savings to checking accounts, have necessitated use of the broader definitions of money supply, such as M2 and M3, in assessing US money supply trends.

An important feature of the nature of money in today's economic systems is that in the United States and most other countries it is not backed by gold, silver, or any other asset. Economists call this "fiat" money. It is a commodity that is declared as money by the central bank, who, as we will see later in this chapter, is authorized to produce it.

**Figure 8-1  US Money Supply**

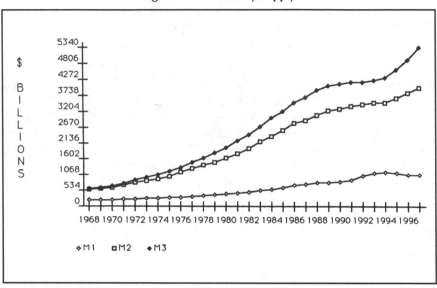

Source: Council of Economic Advisers, *Economic Report of the President, 1998.*

Fiat money has value only because it performs certain functions and therefore is demanded. For example, money is demanded for its value in carrying out economic transactions, as a store of value, and as serving the standard by which relative prices and values of other commodities are judged. Economists call these functions of money transactions demand, asset demand, and the numeraire function. The key to this system working is that the money supply not be allowed to become too great or else, just like any other commodity, the excess supply will bid down the price of money and make it valueless.

## How Money Matters

While the full interactions between the money supply and economic activity are many and complex, we can, as we have repeatedly done before in this guide, draw on the work of the many economists who have examined these interactions and summarize the key relationships in a few principles. In effect, money impacts on a country's economic activity by being the item which is spent to purchase goods and services, including all types of spending. Thus, if more money is available, it is likely that more spending will occur, and if less money is available, then it is likely that less spending will occur.

The specific way a larger money supply impacts on spending is through financial markets. If, for example, more money comes to be in a country's economic system then the presence of the additional money has a tendency to make credit — loans — easier to obtain and interest rates lower. In effect, the increase in the supply of money results in a lower price of money — i.e. a lower interest rate — and more money being demanded — i.e. more borrowing. This greater borrowing then turns into more aggregate demand and, in turn, results in the impacts discussed in Chapter 4 of higher real GDP and more inflation. Conversely, less money/credit in a country's economic system will cause higher interest rates, less borrowing, lower aggregate demand, and lower real GDP and inflation. It is these economic principles that the US central bank — the Federal Reserve System — uses to affect trends in US real GDP and inflation.

## The Federal Reserve System

Before getting into how the Federal Reserve changes the money supply to set off the impacts discussed in the previous section, it will be useful to discuss the institutional aspects of the Federal Reserve. The Federal Reserve began in 1913 when Congress set it up with the explicit purpose of managing the US money supply to try to head off more of the financial crises that had plagued the US economy in the late 1800s and early 1900s.

Today, the Federal Reserve has three main institutional pillars and a variety of functions.

- Twelve Federal Reserve district banks service and oversee commercial banking activities in twelve Federal Reserve regions. These district banks are in Boston, New York, Philadelphia, Richmond, Atlanta, Dallas, Cleveland, St. Louis, Minneapolis, Chicago, Kansas City, and San Francisco. Their main functions are, along with the Federal Deposit Insurance Corporation (FDIC) and other Federal financial regulatory institutions, to oversee and regulate the activities of banks in their region. They also carry out the routine, but important, function of clearing checks. This function can be verified by inspecting the back of a check you write to someone whose bank is in another Federal Reserve region; among the stamps on the back of the check should be the stamps of the Federal Reserve bank in the recipient's region and of the Federal Reserve bank in whose region your bank is located.

- The Board of Governors of the Federal Reserve System — located in Washington DC — is the most important entity in the Federal Reserve System. It is this entity that has the responsibility of setting overall monetary policy — expansionary or contractionary — and other financial regulatory policies, such as so-called margin requirements for the purchase of stocks. The Board is made up of seven individuals, mostly economists or bankers, appointed by the President with the consent of the Senate, to very long terms of 14 years each. The length of the terms is designed to make the Federal Reserve independent of political influence and, hopefully, allow the Board to implement the "best" and not the most politically-expedient monetary policy. This objective has largely been met, as studies indicate the Federal Reserve System is among the more independent (of political pressure) central banks in the world, along with the German Bundesbank and Switzerland's central bank. Separate to the nominations to 14-year terms of regular members, one of the seven members is nominated to a 4-year term as chairman.

- The final main entity in the Federal Reserve System is the Federal Open Market Committee (FOMC). The FOMC implements the monetary policy that the Board of Governors sets by buying and selling government securities on the open market; how this action changes monetary policy will be discussed in the next section. The membership of the FOMC is made up of the Board of Governors and the presidents of five of the regional Federal Reserve Banks. Four of these presidents rotate on and off the FOMC, but the President of the New York Federal Reserve Bank is always on the FOMC because of his/her bank being located in the New York financial center of the United States. Figure 8-2 summarizes the various components and functions of the Federal Reserve system.

## How the Federal Reserve Implements Monetary Policy

In implementing monetary policy, the Federal Reserve builds on the fact that changes in the money supply affects interest rates, aggregate demand,

**Figure 8-2 Federal Reserve: Key Components and Functions**

| Component | Functions |
|---|---|
| District Banks | Oversee Banks<br>Clear Checks |
| Board of Governors | Decides on monetary policy |
| FOMC | Implements monetary policy through open market operations |

Figure 8-3  Changes in US Money Supply (M2)

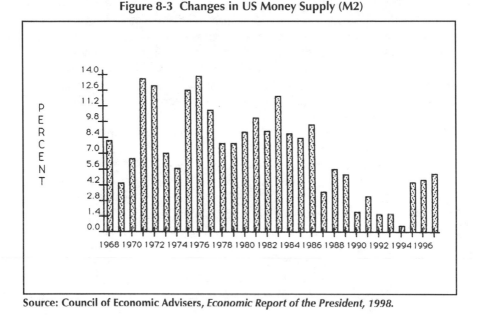

Source: Council of Economic Advisers, *Economic Report of the President, 1998.*

and overall economic performance of the economy. In particular, it utilizes the fact that an increased money supply — an expansionary monetary policy — spurs economic activity and the fact that a lowered money supply — contractionary monetary policy — slows down inflation. Accordingly, when the economy is in recession, the Federal Reserve usually will respond with an expansionary policy, and when the economy is experiencing too much inflation, it will respond with a contractionary policy.

When the October 1987 stock market crash created substantial fear that the collapse would lead to a major US economic recession, the Federal Reserve engaged in an expansionary policy to put more money in the economy to make it easier for entities to keep spending and offset the recessionary policies. Conversely, in the late 1970s, early 1980s, and early 1990s, the Federal Reserve identified inflation as the major problem and put in place contractionary policies to combat it. Figure 8-3 shows how these policies impacted on the money supply.

Once the particular stance of monetary policy — expansionary or contractionary — has been chosen, the Federal Reserve has three tools which it uses to actually bring about a change in the supply of money in the economy — open market operations, changes in the discount rate, and changes in reserve requirements. Of the three, by far the dominant one is used is open market operations, followed by changes in the discount rate. Changes in reserve requirements have occurred, but almost never as a tool of monetary policy.

## Open Market Operations

Open market operations consist of purchases or sales of government securities by the Federal Reserve on financial markets. In an expansionary monetary policy, when the Federal Reserve wants the money supply to rise, it buys securities and increases the money supply as it pays for the securities. In a contractionary monetary policy, the Federal Reserve sells government securities, and as it is paid for the securities causes the money supply to decrease.

In each case, interest rates are also affected. In the case of the expansionary monetary policy, interest rates fall as the increased demand of the Federal Reserve for the securities bids their price up and their yield, or current interest rate, down. In the case of the contractionary policy, an opposite result for interest rates occurs. This connection is often one of the most heavily discussed impacts of changes in monetary policy, with commentators referring to a "rise of half a percentage point in government bond yields as a result of recent actions by the Federal Reserve."

When the Federal Reserve is carrying out monetary policy, it is buying or selling the government securities from private holders, in effect the groups discussed in Chapter 7 as the purchasers of the national debt. In practice, the Federal Reserve does not know who it is buying from or selling to, since, as when an individual buys or sells stock, the transaction is done through a broker, and the identity of the buyer or seller is not known. In practice, it also does not matter who the buyer or seller is in terms of achieving the desired impact on the money supply.

In the case of an expansionary monetary policy, for example, potential sellers of government securities to the Federal Reserve could be a bank or a non-bank economic entity. If the seller is a bank, the sale of the security will give the bank unused funds. Since banks make no money on unused funds, a strong incentive will exist for them to loan the funds out, which will add to the money supply and lower interest rates, the desired result. If the seller is a non-bank, presumably it will either spend the newly acquired funds directly, producing the desired increase in spending, or it will put them in the bank, which will enable the bank to increase its loans and begin the cycle discussed in the previous sentence. In the case of a contractionary policy, an opposite chain of events results.

## Discount Rate

A second monetary policy tool — of somewhat lesser importance than open market operations — is for the Federal Reserve to change the discount rate. The discount rate is the rate that the Federal Reserve charges commercial banks on funds it loans them, chiefly for the purpose of helping them on a short-term basis keep their reserve position in balance. A lower discount rate will encourage banks to borrow more from the Federal Reserve and keep their own loans high, a chain of events that

**Figure 8-4  US Discount Rate Trends**

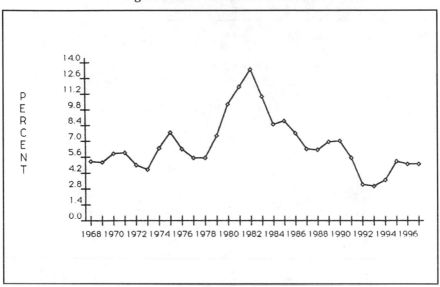

Source: Council of Economic Advisers, *Economic Report of the President, 1998.*

will produce a higher money supply. A higher discount rate will produce the opposite result.

So, to help implement an expansionary monetary policy, the central bank will typically lower the discount rate; to help implement a contractionary monetary policy, it will raise the discount rate. This connection of the discount rate to monetary policy can be seen in Figure 8-4, which shows trends in the discount rate and how they rose during the contractionary monetary policy period of the early 1980s. Figure 8-5 summarizes the process by which open market operations and discount rate changes lead to increases in the nation's money supply and lower interest rates.

### Reserve Requirements

The last potential tool of monetary policy is changes in reserve requirements; however, this tool is almost never used as a tool of monetary policy. Reserve requirements are the mandated percentage of its deposits that a bank must keep in reserve, either as cash in the vault or on deposit at its Federal Reserve bank. This percentage is usually in the 10-15 percent range, a range higher than is probably really necessary, given that patterns of deposits and withdrawals at a reasonably-sized financial institution suggests that 5 percent or so will be sufficient to have enough cash on hand for probable withdrawals.

**Figure 8-5 How Open Market Operations and Discount Rate Changes Affect Money Supply and Interest Rates**

Expansionary Monetary Policy

Open Market Operation:    Federal Reserve Buys Government Securities
Purchases of Government Securities Drive Security Prices Up
Rise In Security Prices Drives Interest Rates Down
Private Owners of Securities Sell Securities And Receive Money
Combined, The Open Market Operation Has Reduced Interest Rates And Increased Money Supply

Discount Rate Change:    Federal Reserve Lowers Discount Rate
Lower Discount Rate Increases Incentives For Banks To Borrow From Federal Reserve
Increased Funds Held By Banks Increases Incentives For Banks To Make More Loans
Increased Loans Increase Money Supply and Lower Interest Rates

Contractionary Monetary Policy

Open Market Operation:    Federal Reserve Sells Government Securities
Sales of Government Securities Drive Security Prices Down
Fall In Security Prices Drive Interest Rates Up
Private Owners of Securities Buy Securities And Give Up Money
Combined, The Open Market Operation Has Raised Interest Rates And Decreased Money Supply

Discount Rate Change:    Federal Reserve Raises Discount Rate
Higher Discount Rate Decreases Incentives For Banks To Borrow From Federal Reserve
Decreased Funds Held By Banks Decreases Incentives For Banks To Make More Loans
Decreased Loans Decrease Money Supply and Raise Interest Rates

If reserve requirements were used as a tool of monetary policy, they would be lowered in association with an expansionary policy to encourage more lending by the bank, and raised in association with a contractionary policy to encourage, indeed force, less lending by the bank. In practice, reserve requirements have almost never been changed for this reason, although they are periodically adjusted to reflect structural changes in the economy and financial system.

## The Impacts of Monetary Policy

Most economists believe that monetary policy is an exceptionally powerful force in determining the overall course of an economy. In particular, many — often called monetarists — think it is far more powerful than fiscal policy.

Using the theoretical framework constructed in Chapter 4, the impacts can be outlined in a relatively straightforward manner.

- An expansionary monetary policy will increase the money supply, lower interest rates and cause an increase in aggregate demand.

- The increase in aggregate demand will raise real GDP and lower unemployment, the desired result, but also will increase inflationary pressures.

- The increase in aggregate demand and the lowered interest rates also will cause deterioration in the country's balance of payments and/or depreciation in its exchange rate, as the increase in economic activity and inflation raises imports and the lower interest rates cause increased net capital outflows.

A contractionary monetary policy will produce opposite results.

- An contractionary monetary policy decreases the money supply and raises interest rates and cause a decrease in aggregate demand.

- The decrease in aggregate demand decreases inflationary pressures, the desired result, but also lowers real GDP and raises unemployment.

- The decrease in aggregate demand and raised interest rates also will cause improvement in the country's balance of payments and/or appreciation in its exchange rate, as the decrease in economic activity and inflation lowers imports and the higher interest rates causes increased net capital inflows.

A particularly powerful linkage between the money supply and inflation seems to exist. For example, almost every case of rapid inflation has been associated with rapid money supply growth, and, conversely, almost all cases of slow inflation have been associated with slow money supply growth.

As with fiscal policy, the internationalization of investment capital markets also has impacts on monetary policy. However, unlike fiscal policy, which international capital flows make more effective, internationalization of capital flows makes monetary policy less effective because when monetary policy tries to change interest rates in order to change aggregate demand, one of the results is for an international flow of capital that works against the intended result. For example, an expansionary monetary policy works in part by bringing down interest rates. However, when the interest rate starts to fall, one of the outcomes will be a capital outflow, which, in turn, will restrict the fall in interest rates.

## Examples of Monetary Policy at Work

Numerous examples can be found that show in the real world how the application of the various monetary policy stances produce the suggested result; some of these examples have already been discussed in the case of the United States.

Another example is Germany following re-unification of West and East Germany. There, the economic situation that faced the Bundesbank — Germany's central bank — was large increases in government spending and a large budget deficit associated with the economic costs of re-unification. The Bundesbank was concerned that this situation would cause a surge of inflation — a sensitive area for Germany given the hyperinflation they suffered in the 1920s and just after World War II.

The Bundesbank met this situation with a contractionary monetary policy. The results were as predicted: inflation was kept under control, but interest rates soared, real GDP growth slowed, unemployment rose, capital inflows increased, and the German mark came under strong pressure to appreciate (see Figure 8-6). The mark did not actually appreciate because of additional actions by the Bundesbank which led to no currency appreciation but to a buildup in German international reserves. This outcome occurred because the Bundesbank carried out foreign exchange market intervention to keep the value of the mark fixed, a central bank activity discussed next.

## Foreign Exchange Market Intervention

Another important role of the central bank in countries with fixed exchange rates for their currency is foreign exchange market intervention to keep the exchange rate fixed. Specifically, if a fixed exchange rate comes under pressure to appreciate or depreciate, then it is the central bank that prevents the actual appreciation or depreciation from occurring, through foreign exchange market intervention.

The way the central bank carries out these preventive steps is to buy or sell the nation's currency on foreign exchange markets in a way that offsets the pressure to appreciate or depreciate. If a currency is under pressure to depreciate, which occurs when the country's balance of payments is in overall non-official deficit, the central bank will buy the excess supplies of the currency to increase demand for the currency and offset the pressure to depreciate. It will have to use its official international reserves, usually foreign exchange, to carry out this buying action and, in turn, will steadily deplete its reserves as long as it is intervening. Central banks often support exchange market intervention by raising interest rates to induce capital inflows and reduce the need to intervene.

**Figure 8-6 Germany: Selected Economic Trends**

|  | 1989 | 1990 | 1991 | 1992 |
|---|---|---|---|---|
| Budget Deficit (DM billions) | -4 | -40 | -67 | -74 |
| Interest Rates (percent) | 6.6 | 7.9 | 8.8 | 9.4 |
| Net Capital Flows ($ billion) | -54 | -38 | 15 | 54 |
| Change in Reserves ($ billions) | 3 | 8 | -5 | 29 |

Source: International Monetary Fund, *International Financial Statistics, Yearbook 1993.*

On the other hand, if a currency is under pressure to appreciate, the central bank is in a stronger position. In this case, what it must do is sell its currency to increase the supply of it on foreign exchange markets and thereby offset the appreciating pressure. This action results in accumulation of international reserves. Because it can supply as much of its own currency as necessary — since it "prints it" — the central bank can continue this type of intervention virtually indefinitely.

Since it went to floating exchange rates in 1971, the United States has seldom carried out foreign exchange intervention, although it did so for a period in early 1995, using its international reserves of Japanese yen to buy dollars to slow the dollar's depreciation below the Y100/$ mark. With the increased capabilities of private investors and speculators to move funds around the world, the ability of central banks to maintain fixed exchange rates when their currencies come under pressure has been dramatically reduced, as attested to by the numerous currency depreciations forced on East Asia and Russia in 1997 and 1998.

## Foreign Exchange Controls

While the United States and most major trading nations chiefly use foreign exchange market intervention to keep exchange rates fixed, many smaller countries in the Third World utilize something called foreign exchange controls to deal with balance of payments imbalances, most often deficits. In essence, these countries require, under force of law, that all foreign exchange entering the country to be sold to the central bank at some, usually overvalued, domestic exchange rate. The central bank then uses its monopoly position — i.e. sole seller — in foreign exchange to re-sell the limited supplies back to domestic citizens wanted at an inflated price. While this system does achieve "balance" in the country's international exchange transactions, it causes huge inefficiencies, corruption, and waste and usually leads to development of an illegal, or black, market for foreign exchange. Despite the disadvantages, interest in exchange controls increased in 1998.

## Summary

1.  Monetary policy involves a nation's central bank altering the supply of money and credit and interest rates to achieve changes in real GDP and inflation.

2.  In the United States, the name of the central bank that carries out these policies is the Federal Reserve System. The Federal Reserve System was set up by Congress in 1913 and is composed of twelve regional banks, a Board of Governors, and the Federal Open Market Committee (FOMC).

3.  The Federal Reserve has a number of functions, such as clearing checks and overseeing and regulating banks, but its chief role is through its monetary policy to manage the nation's money supply in a way that produces desired economic trends.

4.  The Federal Reserve implements monetary policy by changing the supply of money. Because there are strong connections between the supply of money — i.e., coin, currency, demand deposits, saving deposits and money market fund balances — and spending, changes in the supply of money affect overall aggregate demand and, through it, overall trends in real GDP and inflation. Increases in the money supply boost aggregate demand and decreases in the money supply lower aggregate demand.

5.  When the Federal Reserve wants the money supply to rise, called an expansionary or loose monetary policy, which it usually wants to occur during a recession, it increases the money supply by buying government securities on the open market, lowering the discount rate, and, very rarely, lowering reserve requirements. These actions, working through financial markets, produce higher supplies of money and lower interest rates.

6.  When the Federal Reserve wants the money supply to fall or grow more slowly, called a contractionary or tight monetary policy, which it usually wants to occur during a time of too much inflation, it decreases the money supply by selling government securities on the open market, raising the discount rate, and, very rarely, raising reserve requirements. These actions, working through financial markets, produce lower supplies of money and higher interest rates.

7.  The overall results of an expansionary monetary policy are lower interest rates, higher real GDP, lower unemployment, higher inflation, and deterioration in the balance of payments and/or a weaker exchange rate, depending whether the exchange rate is fixed or floating.

8. The overall results of a tight monetary policy are higher interest rates, lower real GDP, higher unemployment, lower inflation, and improvement — i.e. movement toward surplus — in the balance of payments and/or a stronger exchange rate, again, depending on whether the exchange rate is fixed or floating.

9. The internationalization of investment capital markets has made it harder for central banks to pursue monetary policies independent from other countries, because when they try to change interest rates to change aggregate demand, investment capital flows in and out of the country in a way that frustrates the intended policy.

10. Another role of the central bank occurs in a situation when the exchange rate is fixed. In this situation, the central bank will carry out foreign exchange market intervention operations to keep the exchange rate fixed. If the exchange rate is having a tendency to weaken, it will use its official international reserves to buy up its own currency and keep the exchange rate up. In doing so, it will deplete its reserves. If the exchange rate is tending to appreciate, the central bank will sell its own currency, buy up foreign exchange, and keep its exchange rate down. In doing so it will accumulate reserves. Central banks also often support intervention by raising interest rates to draw in foreign capital.

11. While the United States and most major trading nations do not use this method, some Third World countries use exchange controls to deal with balance of payments imbalances. These controls do permit a country to keep control of payments imbalances but generally at huge cost of economic inefficiency and corruption.

# 9 | US and International Trade Patterns

Another important indicator of a country's international economic situation is its pattern of trade — i.e., what products it exports and imports. To describe the pattern of a nation's trade, economists often make use of trade balances in each product or product group. In some products, a given country will have a deficit, and in other products it will have a surplus. For another country, the deficits and surpluses will be in different sets of products. For products in which a country has a trade surplus, the country is seen as competitive; for products where a deficit is present, as uncompetitive.

According to Figure 9-1:

- the United States is a major net exporter of commercial aircraft and agricultural products and a major importer of electronically-based manufactured goods and oil;

- Japan exports a variety of manufactured products and imports food and raw materials;

- China exports a variety of labor-intensive manufactured products and imports wheat and capital equipment;

- and Mexico exports petroleum, agricultural products, and cars and imports a number of manufactured products, including car parts.

Mexico's import of car parts and export of cars is an example of the trade impacts of the globalization of world production that will be discussed in Chapter 12, with foreign automobile companies importing car parts into Mexico for assembly and export as finished cars.

Moreover, not only are there differences in international trade patterns, but these patterns often change. As Figure 9-2 shows, for example, East Asia's share of world exports rose sharply between 1985 and 1995, while other countries', mostly in Latin America, Africa, and the Middle East, shares fell.

### Figure 9-1  Selected Countries: Exports and Imports

| | Exports | Imports |
|---|---|---|
| United States | aircraft, plastics, corn, tobacco, soybeans | petroleum, cars, textiles, shoes, toys |
| Japan | cars, telecommunication equipment, transistors, computers, recorders | petroleum, textiles, agriculture products |
| Germany | cars, industrial machinery, chemicals, | textiles, petroleum, computers, fruit |
| Mexico | petroleum, cars, agricultural products | car parts, industrial machinery, telecommunications equipment |
| South Korea | textiles, ships, shoes, cars, transistors | petroleum, aircraft, chemicals |
| China | textiles, shoes, toys | chemicals, wheat, aircraft, telecommunications equipment |

**Source: Various sources.**

### Figure 9-2  Changes in Shares of Total World Exports

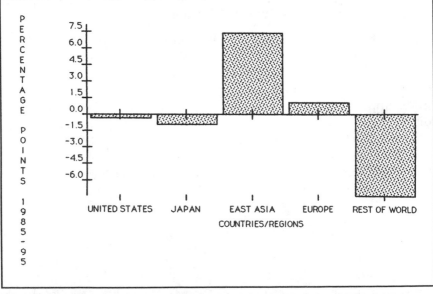

**Source: International Monetary Fund, *International Financial Statistics, Yearbook 1996*.**

## Explaining Trade Patterns

Economists believe trade patterns, and the changes in them, are not accidental, but result from fundamental economic forces. Specifically, economists believe the pattern of a nation's trade is driven by the same type of forces that drives other economic trends — a combination of supply, demand, and the desire of producers to obtain the highest sales and lowest production costs. Putting these theories into operation against observed patterns of trade — whether today, 10 years ago, or 200 years ago — has allowed economists to develop a set of principles to explain patterns of trade.

### *Principle 1.*

*International trade and its patterns are essentially driven by differential holdings of economic resources* — i.e., items such as raw material, labor, technology, capital equipment, etc. that are used in producing products.

Figure 9-1 can be used to illustrate this principle. In effect, the reason for the differing patterns of exports and imports of the countries in this table is the fact that they have different holdings of the economic resources used in the production of economic goods and services. Some have an abundance of labor resource, others an abundance of technology resources, others an abundance of natural resources.

- The fact that the United States exports commercial aircraft and wheat is based on its large holdings of the economic resources of technology and cropland. Conversely, other countries have comparative advantages in the products the United States imports.

- Japan's exports of manufactured goods is due to high levels of the physical capital resources used for these products. Conversely, Japan imports oil and food products because it has a comparative disadvantage in resources needed for these products.

- China's exports of textiles is driven by the fact that it has abundant and low cost amounts of the low skilled labor needed to make textiles. Its imports of manufactured products are driven by the fact that, while China could conceivably make these products, it does not have the best resources in the world for doing so, and therefore cannot produce them as cheaply as other countries.

### *Principle 2.*

*Countries will be net exporters of products in which they have relative abundance of the resources which produce those products and will be net importers of other products.* If a country has relative abundance of resources for producing a product, it will be able to produce the product cheaper than elsewhere in the world, assuming transportation costs and other barriers are minimal, sell that product in other markets more cheaply than other producers. Thus, Brazil exports coffee because its climate enables it to produce coffee more cheaply than elsewhere, Saudi Arabia exports oil because its oilfields produce oil at 4 cents a gallon, Japan exports automobiles because it has the world's best capital equipment and technology for producing automobiles, China exports toys and textiles because these products are highly labor intensive and China has labor in abundance, and the United States exports grain because of the grain-growing advantages of the US Middle West. Also, the United States is a major net exporter of services — technology, insurance, financial, accounting, etc. —because of a strong US competitive advantage in those areas.

It is not necessary that a country have an absolute advantage in producing a product in order for it to export that product, merely that it have a comparative advantage. In other words, the United States may be more efficient than China in producing both capital equipment and textiles, but if the US efficiency edge is greatest in capital equipment, the natural market forces of businesses trying to find low-cost production, high-sale market locations will, even in only a comparative advantage situation, lead to US exports to China of capital equipment and Chinese exports to the United States of textiles.

An analogy at the individual level to this principle of comparative advantage would be an individual who is both an excellent mechanic and an excellent doctor and another person who is a good mechanic but possesses no medical skills at all. Using the terms of the previous paragraph, the first individual has an absolute advantage both in being a mechanic and a doctor. But, it would not make sense for him/her to give up time being a doctor to do mechanical work on his/her car. Rather, it is most efficient for this individual to focus on the activity which he/she has greatest comparative advantage in — being a doctor — and hire out the mechanical work on his/her car. And so it is for countries.

### Principle 3.

*In today's world, the advantage in producing a particular product is not always "given", but is often "created".* In other words, it is possible for nations to change the products in which they have a comparative advantage by accumulating the economic resources that produce those products.

When economic activity was driven more by natural resources, the "creation" of comparative advantage was of course difficult; the nation either possessed the necessary raw materials or it did not. However, in today's world, where economic activity is driven more by technology (see also Chapter 12), it is very possible for countries through investment and research and development to acquire a comparative advantage where they did not have one previously.

This "creation" of comparative advantage has gone on in a number of countries, and, as a result, their trade patterns have changed. And, since comparative advantage is a relative thing, as their comparative advantage has increased, other countries have seen a diminishment in their comparative advantage in those products. For example:

- From the late 1970s to the early 1990s, Japan went from exporting low-technology, labor-intensive products to exporting high-technology products, as did South Korea.

- Over the same period, Malaysia went from exporting tropical agricultural products to exporting manufactured products.

- As these nations have built up comparative advantage in these areas, the United States has seen its share of the world high-technology products market reduced below what it would have been had these other countries not created comparative advantages in various products.

In all of the cases, these countries which created comparative advantage have done so by high rates of investment and research and development in the resources which produce those products.

*Principle 4.*
*The presence of the ability for nations to trade with each other conveys huge productivity gains for the world economy.* Because trade allows, on a global scale, production of each product to "migrate" to the location where it can be produced most efficiently, the world at large achieves huge gains in productive efficiency. Put another way, because coffee consumed in the United States can be grown in Brazil and the computers used in Brazil can be produced in the United States, both countries achieve large gains in overall production efficiency as the United States does not have to strain inappropriate resources to grow coffee and Brazil does not have to try to match the capabilities of IBM or Apple to produce computers.

## Interaction of International Trade and International Investment

Another important trend in today's global economy is the interaction between international trade and foreign direct investment — i.e., a company establishing production facilities in a country other than its own. When trade theory was first developed, international foreign direct investment flows were small, and trade theory therefore assumed, mostly correctly, that exports of a given country were produced by that country's comparative advantage being utilized by producers indigenous to that country. For example, the initial use of trade theory would assume the exports of, say, Malaysia, were produced by Malaysia firms.

Obviously the world has changed dramatically from that assumption. Today, foreign direct investment flows are extremely large. In the 1990s, China alone has received more than $30 billion a year in foreign direct investment inflows. Many other countries, such as Mexico, Hungary, the Czech Republic, Thailand, Malaysia, and Singapore, also have received large amounts of foreign direct investment inflows from countries such as the United States, Japan, South Korea, Taiwan, Hong Kong, and Germany.

The production facilities that these investment flows create complicate the assessment of trade patterns. For example, many of the exports from Singapore are from US-owned factories — are these exports Singaporean or US? Many of the exports from Malaysia and Thailand are from Japan-owned factories — are these exports Malaysian and Thai or Japanese? Since trade data is still compiled on a national geographic basis, exports from a country are counted as that country's exports, regardless of whose company produced and exported them. Yet, these foreign-direct-investment-produced exports clearly are somewhat different.

The main impact foreign direct investment has on international trade is to speed the creation of comparative advantage and to accentuate the natural comparative advantages of a country. China in the late 1980s and early 1990s is a good case study of this impact. China, because of its large population and low incomes, has a large comparative advantage in the production of labor intensive products. Even without foreign direct investment flows, this advantage would eventually have been utilized once China shifted from planned socialism to its brand of capitalism. However, because of the $30 billion a year direct investment inflows, this potential comparative advantage became an actual comparative advantage far quicker.

Foreign direct investment has become a major part of the international economy. In doing so, it has had a major impact on what countries — defined geographically — have comparative advantages in what products. In particular, the process of foreign direct investment has enabled developed country companies to pair their technological expertise with the low labor costs of developing countries to dramatically enhance the comparative advantages of the developing countries, boost the exports and economies of these countries, provide world consumers with more and lower cost products, and enhance their companies' profits.

## Impacts of International Trade on Particular Groups

Principle 4 above — that international trade, whether caused by "given" or "created" comparative advantage, is beneficial — is true, and is one of the enduring dogmas of economics. However, the principle is incomplete in that it does not differentiate the impact of trade for particular groups within economies, and there are several different groups that are impacted.

- One group is consumers — individuals who consume products but do not directly engage in the production of products that are potentially tradeable on an international scale. With the changes in the global economy described in Chapter 12, this group is getting smaller and smaller, but in most countries is still probably a majority of the total economy and population in most countries. Specific occupations likely falling in this category include teachers, government workers, and providers of services such as medical, legal, trade, and distribution.

- Another group is producers of products that are actually or potentially tradeable on an international scale. In this group are most producers of physical goods, ranging from agricultural products through the highest-technology products, and many services which can be delivered internationally. Included in this latter category are many professional services such as accounting, financial, and construction management.

Within these groups, international trade creates two sets of "winners" — i.e. individuals and producers for which international trade clearly is beneficial — and one set of "losers" — i.e. individuals and producers for which international trade is not so clearly beneficial, and may in fact be harmful.

The clearest winners are those producers who, for their product, are among the world's most efficient producers. For them, international trade moves their market from their own country, which it would be in the absence of international trade, to the world, and, in doing so, multiplies immensely their sales and profits.

In the United States, the winners from international trade include firms like Boeing, IBM, Apple, and US grain farmers. In Brazil, a winner is its coffee industry; in Germany, the heavy industrial equipment industry; in France, wine producers; in China, toy manufacturers. In each case, the winning occurs because, given the global distribution of economic resources, each country and industry listed is one of the most efficient, lowest-cost in the world and therefore captures a large part of the world market in the presence of international trade.

A second "winning group" is consumers. This group wins because, with the existence of international trade, they acquire a wider variety of products at lower prices. For example, because international trade enables coffee produced in Brazil to come to the United States, US coffee drinkers get a far better quality of coffee at far lower prices than if that coffee were grown in the United States. Similarly, US automobile buyers get a far greater variety of cars at far lower cost than if no automobile imports into the United States were allowed. On the other side, foreign consumers benefit from being able to buy US products — commercial aircraft, computers, grain, etc. For your own judgment as to whether you, as a consumer, benefit from international trade, try to imagine your lifestyle without imports.

Not all groups win, however, and by now you have probably assessed the groups that are not benefitted by world trade. They are of course those producers for given products who are not among the world's most efficient producers. For these groups, made up of both the owners and workers of the businesses, international trade means not a larger market or lower consumer prices, but an increase in competition from foreign producers who can provide the product better or more cheaply. In turn, the domestic producers will either lose sales or must cut their prices and profits to stay competitive with the foreign producers.

In a world where investment capital as well as goods is freely traded internationally, however, the owners/investors of a company can win, even if they are based in locations which have less than the best resources, as these investors can "move" their investments to other countries which do have more advantageous resources. The investors in the former Zenith television company took advantage of this ability by "moving" 80 percent of their work force to Mexico. The original workers in these industries, in contrast, could not so easily move.

So, while international trade creates for each country "winner" consumers and some "winner" producers, it also creates a group of producers, industries, and workers who are not benefited by international trade. In each country, this group includes industries who produce products which use economic resources that other countries have, or have created, in more abundance or at lower cost. For the United States, it includes such diverse industries as textiles, steel, shoes, televisions, video recorders, sugar, and electronic components. For Japan, it includes rice; for Europe, computers; for Latin America, financial services.

In some of the instances, the disadvantage of the US industry, and the associated advantage of other nations, is due to "natural" competitive advantage, as is the case for textiles. Due to the production of textiles being dependent on low-cost, unskilled labor, it is very difficult for US producers to compete with countries like China, India, and Bangladesh, given high US wage levels — unless of course the owners of US textile companies move factories to these other countries, as many have done. In other instances, the disadvantage of the US industry is due to "created" competitive advantages in other nations, such as is the case for video recorders, where focused investment and research and development efforts in Japan and South Korea allowed them to create the most productive processes in the world for these products.

## Net Impacts

Combining the impacts on winners and losers, economists conclude strongly that international trade indisputably produces net gains for the world economy and for the economic system of individual countries. For nearly all countries, economic analyses of the impacts of international trade show that gains for its world-efficient production processes and consumers far outweigh the losses for its less than world-efficient producers.

That said, international trade does create losing groups, as discussed above, and most countries, including the United States, have not done a very good job of creating mechanisms by which some of the gains of the winners are shared with losers. Even without any explicit sharing mechanisms, some industries and individuals who are initially disadvantaged by international trade may eventually see some benefits, through the lower prices they as consumers pay and through the spillover benefits from the gains achieved by the country's world-efficient producers.

However, for many individuals and industries, these gains are a long time in coming and in many cases will never fully offset the initial losses of profits, sales, incomes, and jobs that the initial onslaught of imports brings. Moreover, it is probable that today's large foreign direct investment flows accentuates these impacts, both the positive ones on a country's consumers and efficient industries and the negative ones on its less efficient industries— especially the workers in those industries. Figure 9-3 summarizes the winners and losers from free trade and provides some US examples.

The frequent reaction of the losing groups provides the bridge into the next chapter, for what many of them do is to appeal for their governments for assistance. Very often, this assistance takes the form of one type or another of government interference in free trade, the subject of Chapter 10.

**Figure 9-3 Impacts of Free Trade on Different Groups**

| Group | Impact | US Examples |
|---|---|---|
| Consumers | Benefited | You and Me |
| A Country's Industries Which Have Best In World Resources Used In Those Industries | Benefited | Boeing, Software Companies |
| A Country's Industries Which Have Less Than Best In The World Resources Used In Those Industries | Harmed | Autos, Steel, Textiles |
| Owners/Investors In Industries Who Can Move Operations To Countries With Best Resources For Activities | Benefited | Electronics, Textiles |

## Summary

1. Another indicator of a country's international economic situation is the product pattern of its international trade, i.e., what products it exports and what products it imports. Across the countries involved in international trade, there are wide variations in these patterns.

2. International trade — and the patterns observed — occurs because of differential holdings of economic resources and the differential costs of production these different holdings create.

3. Countries with a relative abundance of economic resources for producing a product will be able to produce that product cheaply and will be a desired production location, while countries with a relative scarcity of those resources will be a relatively high cost and undesirable production location.

4. Countries which hold the better resources on a global scale for producing a particular product will be net exporters of that product and countries which do not have the better resources will be net importers.

5. In today's technology-driven production processes, this comparative advantage is as likely to be created, through investment and research and development, as it is to be given by nature.

6. Large flows of foreign direct investment in today's world economy is an important facet of this comparative advantage creation process — shortening the period in which a country's potential comparative advantage becomes an actual comparative advantage, and accentuating both positive and negative impacts on the participants in international trade.

7. International trade conveys huge overall benefits on the world economy by allowing each product to be produced in that part of the world where it can be produced most efficiently and cheaply.

8. US and other countries' consumers benefit immensely from international trade by being provided a much greater variety of products at much lower prices that would be the case without international trade.

9. In each product area, world-efficient producers also benefit greatly, by being able to sell to markets worldwide instead of only the market of their home country.

10. On the other hand, producers who, for reasons of economic resource unavailability, cost or other factors, are not world-efficient in the production of their product, are hurt by international

trade as what it brings them is increased competition from foreign producers and lower sales, profits, and jobs.

11. Economists agree strongly that the benefits of international trade to a given country's consumers and world-efficient producers far outweigh the harm done to the country's world-inefficient producers.

12. Most countries do a poor job of establishing mechanisms of sharing the gains of the first two groups with the losses of the last group, and losing groups often go to their governments for assistance and protection from foreign producers.

# 10 | Government Interventions in International Trade

As introduced at the end of the last chapter, producers, including owners and workers, who feel they are losing because of international trade have frequently turned to their governments for assistance with or protection from these impacts. To varying degrees, both in the United States and in other nations, governments have been sympathetic to these pleas and have established policies which intervene in international trade patterns and flows to produce more favorable outcomes for these groups.

## How Governments Intervene in International Trade and the Impacts

The manner in which governments intervene in international trade take two general forms. In the first, and oldest, form, they establish barriers to imports. In the second, and the form which is on the upswing in today's world, they provide subsidies to domestic producers.

### Barriers to Imports

Barriers to imports are of three types — tariffs, quotas, and standards or administrative barriers.

### Tariffs

Tariffs are taxes levied on imported products when they enter the country. Most tariffs are fixed at some dollar value — called a specific tariff — or percent of the value of the imports — called an ad valorem tariff, but some, such as the European Union's variable levy on agricultural imports, vary to always keep the cheaper world price for agricultural products higher than the internal European Union price.

### Quotas

Quotas, which over the 1980s became an increasingly widespread form of trade protection, are physical limits on the amount of a product that can be imported into a country. The United States, for example, has a quota that physically limits the quantity of sugar that can be imported into the United States, and Japan has a very low quota on rice imports — zero!

In some cases, quotas are applied by the exporting country under pressure from trading partners who feel they are being harmed by those exports. In this form, the quotas are called Voluntary Restraints on Exports (VREs). Japan has a VRE on its exports of automobiles to the United States, and also has VREs in place for some of its exports to the European Union. Figure 10-1 shows the pattern of VREs in place in 1989.

### Standards and Administrative Barriers

A final form of trade protection — thought to be practiced especially effectively by Japan — is manipulating standards and administrative procedures to keep out imported products. Examples in this area include such practices as inordinately long quarantine periods for imported products, excessive red tape and paper work to obtain permission to import, and internal laws and regulations which, while not prohibiting imports, discriminate against foreign producers.

**Figure 10-1 Voluntary Export Restraints**
**(Number in Place, March 1989)**

| | |
|---|---|
| By Sector | |
| Steel | 50 |
| Agriculture | 51 |
| Automobile | 20 |
| Textiles | 66 |
| Electronic Products | 28 |
| Shoes | 18 |
| Machine Tools | 14 |
| Other | 42 |
| | |
| By Protected Market | |
| European Community | 173 |
| United States | 69 |
| Japan | 13 |
| Other Industrial Countries | 33 |
| Eastern Europe | 1 |
| | |
| By Restrained Exporter | |
| Japan | 70 |
| Korea | 41 |
| Other Industrial Countries | 38 |
| Eastern Europe | 57 |
| Other Developing Countries | 83 |

**Source: International Monetary Fund,** *Issues and Developments in International Trade Policy,* **August 1992.**

## Impacts

Barriers to trade all have essentially the same impacts — they raise prices to the domestic consumer; assist the protected domestic producer and industry by allowing it to obtain higher prices or more sales; reduce world productive efficiency by forcing production away from its most efficient, lowest-cost locations, and harm the foreign producer by reducing its sales or forcing it to lower its own price in order to remain competitive. Barriers to trade also can have negative effects on the larger sphere of relations between countries, as we have seen in the trade tensions between Japan and the United States.

One important difference exists between the impacts of tariffs and quotas, and, as a result of this difference, economists believe that, if trade protection is to be implemented, it should be with a tariff. When an import tariff is levied: the domestic producer obtains more revenue, the foreign producer obtains less revenue, and the government obtains revenue from the tariffs. If, however, an import quota, or a VRE, is substituted for the tariff, the domestic government gets no revenue and some of the revenue increases that result from the higher price caused by the quota go to the foreign producer.

Such an outcome occurred with the VREs on exports of Japanese automobiles to the United States in the 1980s. The quota, and the strong demand for these cars, allowed Japanese automakers to sharply raise their prices — usually seen on the sticker as "Dealer Markup". In fact, the quotas may not have hurt Japanese producers at all, as what they lost in quantity of sales they more than made up in increased revenue per sale. Figure 10-2 summarizes impacts of trade barriers.

## Subsidies

Increasingly, industries are turning to subsidies as a means of obtaining assistance from foreign competition. In general, a subsidy is a payment by the government to a producer for that producer carrying out some particular activity. Subsidies occur not only in international trade. For example, AMTRAK, the US Postal Service, public television, and most higher education in the United States receives government subsidies of one kind or another.

**Figure 10-2  Summary of Impacts of Trade Barriers**

reduces imports
protects domestic producers
raises prices to domestic consumers
reduces sales of foreign producers
reduces economic efficiency
tariffs raise revenue for government
quotas allow some benefits of higher prices to be captured by foreign
 producers

In terms of subsidies that impact the international trade arena, the subsidies take four forms — export, production, technology and export financing.

- Export subsidies are payments to a country's domestic producers for exporting their product. This subsidy allows them to export the product more cheaply and thereby become more competitive. While obviously not a trade barrier, an export subsidy clearly is a government intervention into international trade in that it creates a government-supported advantage for the producers being given the subsidy. At the moment, the United States is providing export subsidies for grains and the European Union regularly provides export subsidies for its farm products.

- Production subsidies are payments to a country's domestic producers for producing their product. While not directly a trade-related activity, the production subsidy causes greater production and, in turn, causes more production to enter world markets to the disadvantage of foreign producers. European Union and US agricultural programs are the major examples of this form of subsidy, and indeed were the big issue in the Uruguay Round of international trade negotiations that was completed in 1993 (see last section in this chapter). Many countries give their producers production subsidies of one form or another.

- Technology subsidies are government payments to a country's domestic producers to assist them in creating a new product or production method. In effect, the government bears the research and development costs. The most visible example of a technology subsidy is the European-made series of airliners called Airbus. In this case, European governments almost fully underwrote the costs of researching and developing this now very large family of airliners which did not exist 20 years ago. However, many other governments practice technology subsidies as well, including the United States where the military-related research and development spending of the Department of Defense has constituted a major technology subsidy to many US companies who have converted results of their government contracts into commercial applications.

- Export financing subsidies are government guarantees on loans to finance exports. These guarantees allow interest rates on such financing to be lower. In the United States, the Export-Import Bank provides these subsidies.

The impacts of subsidies are as follows:

- Foreign producers are disadvantaged as subsidies enable domestic producers to increase their supply of the product at lower costs. Thus, the US export subsidies for grain have a major negative impact on the grain exports of Australia, and European governments' technology subsidy for Airbus has a major negative impact on Boeing.

- The domestic producers receiving the subsidy benefit as they are able to export, produce, or acquire new technology more cheaply as a result of the subsidy. In contrast to the impact on foreign producers, US grain farmers and the European companies that make Airbus are better off as a result of the US grain export and European aerospace technology subsidies.

- Consumers of the products being subsidized benefit from the subsidies because the subsidies cause producers to produce more of the product and to sell it more cheaply. In the case of export subsidies, the benefit goes to foreign consumers, but in the other subsidies — production and technology — all consumers of those products benefit. In the case of the Airbus subsidy, for example, airline passengers now have a wider variety of aircraft to choose from to fly on, probably at lower ticket prices.

- However, there is a price to be paid for the subsidies, and it is the taxes that have to be collected to fund the subsidies. US and European Union agricultural subsidies, for example, each have totalled as much as $20-30 billion a year, funds that have to be raised from the taxpayers. And, non-subsidized producers are harmed, both by having to pay taxes and because of the fact that the lower prices of the subsidized products draw away some of their sales.

- In addition, subsidies diminish world productive efficiency by, like trade barriers, causing production of products to be carried out in parts of the world where it is done less efficiently. Figure 10-3 summarizes the impacts of subsidies.

## Trade Groups

Another way in which governments intervene in international trade, and an important issue in today's world, is by forming trade groups — essentially a number of countries/governments agreeing to eliminate or reduce trade barriers among themselves.

**Figure 10-3 Summary of Impacts of Subsidies**

reduces costs of domestic producers
increases exports and sales of domestic producers
lower prices to consumers
reduces sales of foreign producers
requires taxes to fund subsidies
works against non-subsidized producers, including domestic ones
reduces world productive efficiency

- A free trade area, the nature of the North american Free Trade Agreement (NAFTA) committed to by the United States, Canada, and Mexico, reduces or eliminates tariffs within the free trade area, but each member keeps its own set of tariffs with the rest of the world. In NAFTA, for example, the United States could charge a 20% tariff on imports from products outside of NAFTA, while Canada could charge a 10% tariff.

- A customs union, which was the nature of the trade grouping associated with the European Community, occurs when countries eliminate tariffs with each other and set common tariffs with all other countries. Each European Community member, for example, had no tariffs on any products coming from another European Community member, and exactly the same tariff as each other member on products coming from non-European-Community countries.

- A common market is an extension of a customs union in which all barriers to trade are eliminated. The evolution of the European Community into the European Union in the early 1990s marked a transition for those countries from a customs union to a common market.

While trade groupings are a government intervention into international trade, they are thought by economists to be positive because they generally lower rather than raise trade barriers. The main impacts are to: increase the efficiency of economic activities within the group as the reduced barriers allow a re-allocation of production within the group to the locations it can be done most efficiently; in the beginning to divert imports from countries outside the group to trade within the group as a result of, due to the reduction in barriers, intra-group trade becoming less expensive relative to outside-group trade; and, over time, to enhance imports from non-group countries as increased economic efficiency enables the group to grow more rapidly and to increase imports across the board.

In terms of winners and losers, the initial stages benefit producers within the group at the expense of non-group producers, as a result of the trade diversion effect. Over time, however, the creation of trade that results from the more rapid economic growth of the group may lead to net benefits even to producers even outside of the group. Most observers believe the impact on US producers of the formation of the predecessor of the European Union, the European Community, has been positive, as long-term trade creation effects outweighed initial trade diversion effects.

There are impacts within the group as well, and some of these impacts are negative, as the difficulty in getting US Congressional approval of NAFTA in 1993 attests to. The internal impacts of forming a free trade area are the same as for establishing freer international trade in general. The most efficient producers of given products within the group benefit, consumers benefit, and less-than-most efficient producers within the group are adversely affected.

In the case of NAFTA, these economic principles produced political opposition in Mexico from grain growers and financial institutions who correctly saw themselves as less efficient than US producers of those products and political opposition in the United States from labor unions who saw the products produced by their low and moderate skilled union members having difficulty competing with lower-wage Mexican workers. In terms of jobs, it is important to note that, while the increased efficiency provided by NAFTA likely will increase jobs in both countries, the increases will be on a net basis. More jobs will be created than lost, but some jobs will be lost in both countries.

## Free Trade Zones

Another tool which some governments use in the international trade arena is Free Trade Zones (FTZs), also sometimes called Export Processing Zones (EPZs). FTZs are certain small areas of a country, usually near a seaport or airport, in which normal taxes and regulations are suspended for foreign investors who build factories in the FTZ and agree to direct the production of the factories only to exports.

FTZs often provide substantial benefits to the country by attracting investments, jobs, and technology that might otherwise not have come, while, because of the export only provision, still protecting domestic markets from being disrupted by production from the factories. China has made very successful use of FTZs — called by them Special Economic Zones — as has the Philippines at the former US naval base at Subic Bay.

## The International Trading System

A final important topic to be discussed with regard to government intervention in international trade is the international framework for trade. That framework has been based first on the General Agreement on Tariffs and Trade (GATT), an agreement among nations now numbering more than 100 set up initially in 1947, and, since January 1995, on its successor, the World Trade Organization (WTO). The purpose of these organizations has been to create an international trading system that has no barriers. While by no means fully successful, the GATT and WTO processes have carried the world economy very far in the direction of free international trade, at least compared to the initial situation.

This accomplishment has been reached primarily through several "rounds" of global negotiations with the purpose of reducing tariffs and other trade barriers. The most significant of these rounds were the Dillon Round, the Kennedy Round, the Tokyo Round, and most recently, the Uruguay Round. Each of the earlier rounds led to dramatic reductions in trade barriers, and the implementation of the Uruguay Round agreements will do the same. As a result, these rounds have increased world economic efficiency, benefited consumers and a myriad of most-efficient producers of particular products, but have, at least in the short-run periods following the implementation of each round, disadvantaged less efficient producers.

However, the world trading system, despite the eventual completion of the Uruguay Round — it took from 1986 to 1993 for it to be completed — is under stress. As a result of the difficulties of the Uruguay Round, many countries and regions have gone somewhat their own way. The recent furthering of the economic cohesiveness of the European Union, rumblings about an East Asian trade grouping, and even NAFTA are thought by many observers in part to have occurred because of the Uruguay Round tensions.

Countries also are carrying out unilateral or bilateral actions to a much greater extent than when the GATT seemed to be working better. The numerous VREs forced on Japan are examples of these initiatives, as are the 2-3 dozen trade actions the United States Trade Representative (USTR) is engaged in under so-called Section 301 actions to try to open markets more to US and other countries' imported products. The pressure on Japan and China for greater market access are some prominent examples of these actions.

In part, the WTO that was created in January 1995 was created in response to the difficulties of the Uruguay Round and these regional and bilateral trade deals. The formation of this new organization, agreed to as part of the conclusion of the Uruguay Round, has added to the GATT additional powers and resources to carry out what is called dispute settlement in international trade. In effect, instead of just being able to facilitate trade negotiations, which is what the GATT primarily did, the WTO will be given the powers and resources to investigate and rule on trade differences between nations.

## Summary

1.   Because some groups in countries who engage in international trade are harmed, if not permanently, at least in the short to medium run, governments have intervened in the international trade process to assist or protect these groups.

2.   These interventions have taken two main forms — barriers to imported products and subsidies to domestic producers.

3. Barriers to imports consist of tariffs, quotas — sometimes put on by the exporting country as a VRE — and administrative barriers.

4. These barriers raise prices to domestic consumers, allow protected domestic producers to be more successful, and harm exports of foreign producers. Economists believe that tariffs are preferred over quotas, in part because a share of the higher price that results from the tariff goes to the government in the form of revenue, whereas with a quota it accrues to the foreign producer.

5. Subsidies are payments by the government to a producer for carrying out a specified activity. In the context of international trade, these subsidies take the form of export subsidies, production subsidies, technology subsidies, and export financing subsidies.

6. Subsidies have a number of impacts. In contrast to trade barriers, they benefit consumers by encouraging more production. They also benefit the subsidized firms, but negatively impact foreign producers who now must compete against foreign governments as well as foreign firms. Subsidies also require a tax burden to be placed on the general taxpayer to provide funds for the subsidy.

7. Governments have also intervened in trade in more positive ways, by forming trade groups, either customs unions or common markets, like the European Community/Union in which all countries in the group have free trade with each other and the same external barriers, or free trade areas — like NAFTA — in which countries in the group have lowered tariffs with each other but maintain differing external barriers.

8. Trade groupings are generally thought to: increase the overall efficiency of the countries in the trade group; initially to divert trade away from non-group countries to countries in the group; but over time to create additional trade, even for non-group countries.

9. The formation of a trade group also causes economic impacts within the group, chiefly to shift production from less efficient producers in the group to more efficient producers. It was these shifts, which in the case of NAFTA tended to work to the disadvantage of low and moderate skilled US workers, that made NAFTA such a major US political issue.

10. International trade has occurred under a set of international rules set forth by an international set of agreements called the GATT. The main impact of the GATT has been to sponsor over the past 40-plus years a number of international trade-barrier-reducing negotiations, called rounds, that have substantially reduced the overall level of world-wide tariffs. Less progress has been made

in reducing other types of trade barriers, and the most recent round, the Uruguay Round, was an especially difficult set of negotiations that almost did not reach successful completion.

11. In January 1995, the GATT evolved into the World Trade Organization (WTO). This new organization has additional powers to investigate and resolve trade disputes between nations.

# 11 | Long-Run Economic Growth and Competitiveness

Many of the issues discussed so far in this book relate to how economies' performances vary in the short to medium term. Of equal, and, over the long-run, perhaps even greater, importance are countries' fundamental economic growth and competitiveness trends, for it is these trends that ultimately raise, or do not raise countries' basic living standards.

As noted in Chapter 1, countries' economic performances have varied widely. For example, US real GDP growth per capita (real GDP growth minus population growth) has averaged only about 1.3 percent per year over the past decade, while growth in other countries has been much more rapid (see Figure 11-1).

These differences in growth performances have important implications.

- First, sustained higher real GDP growth dramatically lifts standards of living. The differences in total income gains over a 10-year period

**Figure 11-1  Selected Countries: Real GDP Growth Per Capita, 1985-95 (Percent Per Year)**

| | | | |
|---|---|---|---|
| United States | 1.3 | Western Europe | |
| Japan | 2.9 | France | 1.5 |
| Other East Asia | | Germany | -0.1 |
| South Korea | 7.7 | Italy | 1.8 |
| Malaysia | 5.7 | United Kingdom | 1.4 |
| Singapore | 6.2 | Eastern Europe/Russia | |
| Thailand | 8.4 | Russia | -5.1 |
| Indonesia | 6.0 | Hungary | -1.0 |
| China | 8.3 | Poland | 1.2 |
| Latin America | | Czechoslovakia | -1.8 |
| Argentina | 1.8 | | |
| Brazil | -0.8 | Other Countries | |
| Chile | 6.1 | India | 3.2 |
| Mexico | 0.1 | Nigeria | 1.2 |

Source: *World Development Report, 1997.*

between annual growth of 2.5 percent and 7.5 percent, for example, is 60 percent. These differences are evidenced in the real world in the astounding change in living conditions in South Korea, where real GDP gains over the past 20 years have averaged almost 10 percent a year. On the other hand, slow real output growth allows only slow growth in living standards and real incomes. The stagnation in US real incomes of the past 20 years has been partly due to relatively slow US real GDP growth over that period.

- More rapid economic growth also causes dramatic changes in economies' overall size. For example, because China's economy has grown 9 percent a year since 1978 compared to US growth of only 2.5 percent, China's economy has moved from one-sixth to one-fourth the size of the US economy (see Figure 11-2). If these growth rates continue, China's economy will surpass the US economy in size around 2040.

## Causes of Economic Growth and Competitiveness: Economic Resources

The best place to begin understanding causes of differences in nations' long run economic growth patterns is by remembering the connections between economic output and economic resources discussed in Chapter 3. In effect, the countries which have grown rapidly have done so because they have increased the amount of economic resources they have, especially the resources of human capital, physical capital, financial

Figure 11-2 Selected Economies, Changes in Relative Overall Size
(Billions 1995 US Dollars, Purchasing Power Parities)

|                | 1980 | 1995 |
|----------------|------|------|
| United States  | 4959 | 7248 |
| Japan          | 1689 | 2679 |
| China          | 477  | 2000 |
| Germany        | 984  | 1452 |
| India          | 656  | 1409 |
| Italy          | 824  | 1332 |
| United Kingdom | 915  | 1138 |
| Brazil         | 743  | 977  |
| Indonesia      | 298  | 711  |
| South Korea    | 168  | 591  |
| Thailand       | 132  | 417  |

Source: Central Intelligence Agency, *Handbook of International Economic Statistics, 1996,* and author calculations.

capital, technology, and entrepreneurship. Conversely, countries have slow economic growth because they have not increased their holdings of key economic resources, or have not used their resources efficiently.

Economists have categorized ways in which countries' stocks of various economic resources are increased, and we can use these definitions to better understand how increments to economic resources occur.

- Increases in the labor resource occur as a result of natural population increases, increased labor force participation, or higher levels of immigration.

- A country's holdings of human capital is added to by increased education and training of the country's citizens.

- More physical capital is obtained by increased rates of investment in real capital formation.

- Additional technology resources are obtained by additional research and development (R&D), or by more effectively gaining access to other countries' technology.

- More entrepreneurship occurs when circumstances in a country change in a way that more people are encouraged to start and run private business enterprises.

- Increased amounts of natural resources can be found through increased exploration. In today's world of international trade, however, having indigenous natural resources is not necessary for economic success, since these resources can easily be bought on world markets.

- Finally, it is essential that the domestic financial system be stable and that it effectively provides financing to appropriate, productive investments.

So, the more a given country: educates and trains its population, invests, engages in R&D, accesses foreign technologies, starts businesses, explores for domestic or lines up foreign natural resources, and maintains stable and efficient financial institutions, the more its economic resources and economic capabilities will grow, and the faster real GDP growth it will achieve.

## Economic Policy and Economic Resources

Understanding the connection between economic growth and economic resources is only the first part of the story, however. The second part is understanding that these activities — investment, R&D, education, etc. — that add to economic resources do not just happen. Rather, they are the result of the political, economic, and societal decisions of countries.

In effect, countries that have high levels of physical capital, highly skilled populations, high levels of technology, sound financial capital, and many entrepreneurs have these resources because they have in place economic policies, political climates, and societal mores that encourage these activities. Conversely, countries that do not have them fall short because of present and past deficiencies in their policies and habits. The following paragraphs outline specific policies that economists believe promote the activities that add to countries' economic resources.

### Obtaining a More Highly-Skilled Work Force

Countries that have achieved highly-skilled work forces or rapid increases in their work force's skill levels have done so primarily by devoting large amounts of government expenditures to supporting wide-spread educational and training programs. South Korea, for example, is cited by a World Bank study as having achieved a great part of its economic success through a well-planned program of providing high-quality primary and secondary education to its citizens.

### Achieving High Investment Rates

High investment rates must first of all be underpinned with a high domestic saving rate. Despite the increasing globalization of financial flows to be discussed in Chapter 12, most savers seem to prefer to keep their savings in their own country. Thus, without a high saving rate, it is unlikely that a country will have a high investment rate. A low saving rate is a key factor behind low US investment, and a high saving rate is a chief reason for high Japanese investment (see Figure 11-3).

**Figure 11-3  Investment Rates for United States and Selected Other Countries**

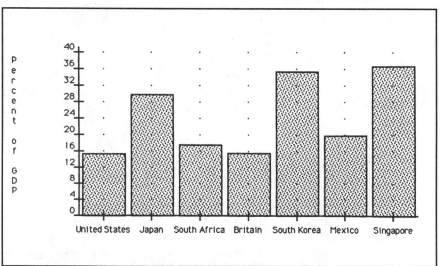

Source: International Monetary Fund, *International Financial Statistics,* August 1998.

Government economic policies play an important role in determining both saving and investment rates. Japan, for example, has savings facilities in its post offices, making it easy for small savers to place their savings into the financial system; for many years excluded investment earnings from taxes, increasing the incentive to save; does not have a strong public social security program; and makes little use of credit cards, which increase borrowing and in turn reduce the net amount of savings available for investment. These characteristics are opposite to the situation in the United States.

Investment itself can also be directly encouraged through the use of special incentive programs, such as investment tax credits, setting up of special financial institutions to channel money to real capital formation. Some examples of these type of efforts in the United States include various investment tax credits that have occasionally been part of the US tax code and the Small Business Administration, which channels money to small businesses. However, if the savings rate is low, all these programs do is re-allocate the existing low amount of savings and investment. They do not fundamentally increase either.

### Achieving Rapid Growth in Technology

Countries achieve rapid growth in their technology resources in two ways — by carrying out indigenous R&D and by encouraging inward flows of technology from the rest of the world, either through licensing agreements or inward foreign direct investment. The United States has achieved its technology gains largely by the first method. Indeed, as the world technology leader for most of the post World War II period, it was only by this method that the United States could obtain its technology gains, since no other country had "better" technology that the United States could obtain. However, that situation has now changed, and the United States does obtain technology through licensing agreements and foreign direct investment into the United States by producers of other countries, notably Japan.

Japan achieved its remarkable technology gains of the past three decades by utilizing both methods. It has a very high R&D rate — now higher than that of the United States — but also made extensive use of licensing agreements to obtain foreign, primarily US, technology. Japan relied very little on inward foreign direct investment to obtain technology.

China is a country that is relying very heavily on foreign direct investment to obtain upgrades to its technology base. When China began its economic takeoff in 1978, it was extremely backward in commercial technologies. To catch up in the quickest way possible, China has encouraged massive inward foreign direct investment. These investments have brought money and jobs also, but most importantly to China, they also have brought advanced commercial technologies.

Indeed, in recent years, China has been exerting the leverage of access to its potentially huge market to "force" inward foreign direct investment.

In one case, China made a contract to purchase aircraft contingent on the seller building an aircraft assembly plant in China.

### Obtaining More Entrepreneurship

The final factor that must grow rapidly in order for a country to achieve rapid economic growth is entrepreneurship, or business sense. In a capitalist, market economic system, it is this resource which allows the economy to make maximum use of the other resources the economy has access to. History has shown that without this resource, even in the presence of ample amounts of other resources, rapid economic growth will not occur. For example, the former USSR had high investment rates, strong R&D efforts, a skilled work force, and immense holdings of natural resources, but its economy failed because its system and policies killed off entrepreneurship.

Conversely, countries that have favored entrepreneurship have had much more favorable economic performances. Indeed, even countries that stifled entrepreneurship for many years through socialist policies and then switched to more capitalist policies quickly saw an "outpouring" of entrepreneurship and much more rapid economic growth. China before and after its 1978 economic reforms, Mexico before and after Carlos Salinas de Gotari became President in 1988, Britain before and after Margaret Thatcher, and to some extent the United States before and after Ronald Reagan's policies of the early 1980s are examples of how a change in policies toward entrepreneurship can bring quick positive results.

### Achieving a Sound Financial System

A final pre-condition to sustained economic progress is a financial system that channels saving and investment of the basis of sound economic criteria. Achievement of such a system is based on strong oversight and supervision of the financial system, openness of the system to competition, and no state owned or favored banks.

## Summary

1.  Ongoing, long-run economic performances of countries differ markedly. For example, over the past decade, real GDP growth in a number of East Asian countries has been triple that of the United States.

2.  Faster growth means faster gains in economic activity, incomes, living standards, and the overall size of a country's economy.

3. Rapid economic growth in a country occurs because that country achieves rapid growth in its holdings of economic resources, especially of human capital, physical capital, technology, entrepreneurship, and financial capital.

4. A government's policies heavily influence the extent to which its country's economy engages in the type of activities that add to economic resources — activities such as investment, education, R&D, and the starting of businesses. Policies that promote investment, R&D, education, and entrepreneurship will lead to more of these activities, increase the rate of economic resource enhancement, and boost the country's economic growth.

# 12 | The New Global Economy

In this final chapter in understanding today's US and global economic trends, we recognize that the basic structure of the world economic system has changed dramatically and examine the implications of those changes. Two decades ago, the world economic system was one in which production was based on natural resources and unskilled labor and national economies were only slightly linked to each other. That situation has changed to one in which national economies are as much international as national with extensive international economic connections in the arenas of trade, investment, ownership, and technology, and one in which the most important resources of production are technology and human capital.

## The Shift to High-Technology, Human-Capital Based Production

The first change that has fundamentally altered the way today's world economies work is the shift from natural resources and low-skilled labor to technology and high-skilled labor as the primary factors of production. This shift can be illustrated at the anecdotal level by noting that if one thinks of the dominant industry in the United States in the 1950s and 1960s, what would come to mind probably would be steel. Indeed, in 1962, steel was so important to the US economy that then President John Kennedy called US steel companies presidents to the Oval Office to lecture them on the need to not increase the price of steel.

In today's world, such an event would be highly unlikely. More likely would be the President calling in, as to some extent has occurred, the presidents of US computer or telecommunication companies, for these are the companies that are the most important and influential companies in the US and world economy today. Steel, meanwhile, has become much less important, as illustrated by the fact that while the US economy is more than twice its size of the late 1960s, its consumption of steel actually is lower. Figure 12-1 presents a broader listing of how the US economy's use of various products has changed over the past couple of decades.

Figure 12-1  Changes in US Economy's Use of Various Products, 1970s-1990s
(Index of Ratio of Use to GDP, 1980=100)

|  | 1980 | 1990 |
|---|---|---|
| Steel | 100 | 79 |
| Oil, Gas, Coal | 100 | 38 |
| Semiconductor Products | 100 | 140 |
| Personal Computers | 100 | 660 |

Source: *Statistical Abstract of the United States, 1993.*

The economic impact of these changes, of course, extends beyond the companies and products involved, for to produce computers and telecommunications equipment instead of steel requires a fundamentally different mix of economic resources. In particular, whereas the process of producing steel relied heavily on natural resources and low-skilled labor, to produce computers and telecommunications equipment requires technology and high-skilled labor.

These changes in the nature of the production process have shifted and continue to shift the fortunes of groups and countries on a global scale. In effect, countries and groups which have the economic resources to produce and utilize technology have gained advantage, while groups which relied on the old style, natural-resource-based production have lost advantage. We can see how these shifts have played out on both a global scale and within the United States.

Globally, countries which were relatively well off in the early 1980s because they had valuable natural resources are now in trouble because those natural resources are no longer so valuable. The most dramatic example of countries like these are the oil producing nations. Because oil is no longer so valuable as an input to the world production process — as evidenced by the fall in its price from $35 per barrel in 1981 to about $12 per barrel today, without even taking account the fact that inflation has made the $12 worth even less — the formerly rich oil producing nations on the Persian Gulf are all now suffering major economic stresses.

In contrast, other countries — those who have the resources to create and utilize technology — have benefited from this shift. These are countries which have highly-skilled, disciplined, motivated work forces. Indeed, a large part of the US economic success in the 1990s can be attributed to the growing importance of technology in production, combined with the exceptional "technology-handling" capabilities of the highly skilled US work force. Figure 12-2 shows how the shift in world production from natural resources to technology has shifted relative real GDP growth rates.

Within the United States, this shift in the nature of production also has impacted, and in particular has been a major factor in the widening of the US income distribution. Before this revolution in the nature of production, demand for US labor across all skill levels rose about equally. Thus, before the mid 1970s, the earnings of both low-skilled and high-skilled US labor rose.

Since the mid 1970s, however, the wages of low-skilled labor have actually declined in real terms because, in a technology-driven world, their type of work is no longer in demand. In contrast, in today's technology-driven world, high-skilled workers are in higher demand, such their wages have continued to rise. Figure 12-3 shows how wages of various groups have changed in response to these shifts.

## The Globalization of Economic Decisions

The second "great" shift that is occurring in today's world economy is the globalization of economic processes. This globalization is occurring at many levels — trade, investment, technology, corporate decision making.
In the case of the United States, for example:

- International trade in economic goods and services now combine to more than 20 percent of total US economic output, nearly double where it was in 1970 (see Figure 12-4). Many US companies, such as Boeing, IBM, and Motorola, rely on foreign countries as markets and production sites for close to 50 percent of their activities.

- The US market for financial capital draws on capital inflows from foreign countries of close to $600 billion a year to fund investment activities that take place in the United States, while US investors place $400 billion worth of investments in other countries.

- Many production facilities in the United States are now owned by foreign companies, such as eight automobile assembly plants in the Midwest owned by Japanese automobile companies.

- Conversely, US companies have placed many of their production facilities abroad, in some cases to produce products for export back to and sale in the United States.

The extent of this integration is evident in a myriad of examples at the level of the individual US consumer. Just go into a clothing store and examine the collar tags that show where the product was made. Most likely you will see a lot of China, Hong Kong, India, El Salvador; most likely you will not see a lot of USA. Or, look at the cars on US roads. Toyotas, Hondas, Nissans, VWs, etc. will be almost as common as Chevrolets, Fords, and Plymouths. Even many US name brands will have been manufactured abroad.

Figure 12-2  Real GDP Growth Rates, before and after Shift from Natural Resource to Technology Driven Production (percent per year)

|  | Prior to 1980 | Since 1980 |
|---|---|---|
| United States | 2.8 | 2.3 |
| Western Europe | 3.0 | 2.3 |
| Saudi Arabia | 11.4 | 1.4 |
| Venezuela | 4.0 | 2.2 |
| South Korea | 8.2 | 9.0 |
| Taiwan | 9.3 | 7.8 |

Source: Central Intelligence Agency, *Handbook of International Economic Statistics,* September 1994.

Figure 12-3  Changes in US Real Wage Rates, after Shift from Natural Resource to Technology Driven Production (percent change, 1983-91)

| Managers | 4.6 |
|---|---|
| Professional Specialists | 8.1 |
| Technical Support | -0.7 |
| Administrative Support | -7.3 |
| Production Line Workers | -6.7 |
| Service Workers | -4.6 |

Source: *Statistical Abstract of the United States, 1992.*

Figure 12-4  United States: Importance of International Trade and Capital Flows

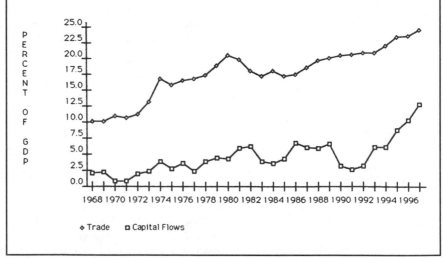

Source: Council of Economic Advisers, *Economic Report of the President, 1998.*

On the other side of the ledger — the sales and activities of US companies in other countries — the illustrative evidence is equally dramatic. The largest McDonalds in the world is in Moscow, the second largest in Beijing. A major US export, for better or worse, are the recordings of Michael Jackson. On the investment side, many even small US investors now are collectively contributing significant amounts of investment capital to foreign countries through international mutual funds such as the Singapore Fund, the Malaysian Fund, the Emerging Mexican Fund, and the Latin American Fund. Scores of mutual funds now focus primarily on foreign investment markets and opportunities.

This increased integration of national economies into a global economic system is no less prevalent in other countries. The economies of Europe are becoming increasingly integrated with each other under the auspices of the European Union (formerly the European Community). The economies of East Asia are integrating with each other, and, under the auspices of the North American Free Trade Agreement (NAFTA), similar trends are occurring in the US, Canadian, and Mexican economies. Figure 12-5 shows the internationalization of selected foreign economies.

**Figure 12-5 Non-US Economies: Foreign Trade in Relation To GDP, 1997 (Combined exports and imports of goods and services as percent of GDP)**

| | |
|---|---|
| Japan | 21 |
| Germany | 50 |
| Mexico | 60 |
| South Korea | 77 |
| Singapore | 144* |
| India | 21 |
| Brazil | 16 |

*Singapore is what is known as an entropot economy, i.e., one which relies heavily on foreign trade. The reason Singapore's exports and imports exceeds its actual production is that much of its trade simply passes through the country.

Source: International Monetary Fund, *International Financial Statistics*, August 1998.

The growing integration of the world's national economies into a global economy is occurring in four areas: trade, investment, ownership, and technology.

- World trade now amounts to near 20 percent of total world economic output, up from only 8 percent in 1965, with increasing proportions of this trade being accounted for by intra-company trade — i.e., trade between units of the same corporation. For example, 40 percent of US imports from Singapore consist of US corporations exporting the output of their Singapore factories back to the United States for sale or further processing.

- The internationalization of investment has grown even more rapidly. The amount of cross-national-border investment relative to world economic activity has jumped by a factor of 20 from 1980 to the present. As to the impact of this phenomenon on the United States, in the late 1980s, foreign investors provided funds that financed one-third of US government budget deficits, while, going the other way, US banks provided hundreds of billions of dollars of loans to companies and governments in Latin America during the 1980s.

- Cross-border ownership connections, chiefly in the form of joint ventures between a foreign investor and a domestic company, also have grown dramatically. In the United States, for example, many US auto companies have formed joint ventures with Japanese companies, and the Kuwait Finance Corporation is a major investor in the Kiawah Island Resort development in South Carolina.

- Finally, technology increasingly is shared across national borders by companies who feel that by sharing each other's technology, they both can derive benefit. In the Boeing 777 airliner, for example, much of the electronic content is being derived from such arrangements between Boeing and Japanese electronic companies.

## Causes of Global Economic Integration

This increased global economic integration has largely been driven by the decisions and actions of private business, both US and foreign. They have carried out this international linking of their economic activities on this global scale in search of two objectives that bear heavily on their profits — markets and lower costs. If a business, whether based in the United States or elsewhere, can expand its market, it will sell more and increase its profits, and, if a business can find a lower-cost way, or place, to produce its profits, it again will increase its profit.

While the above paragraph is clearly valid, it does not fully explain why the surge in international economic linkages has been a phenomenon of the past decade or so and did not occur earlier. For the answer to that question, developments in two areas — technological advances and changes in government policies — need to be examined. Both have been vital to the increased integration of the world economy.

### The Technology Factor

In the technology area, advances in three specific sectors have been most important in underpinning increased global economic integration. For any business, three activities are essential for multi-location marketing and production: ease of transport of material and finished products among the company's production locations and markets; ease of communication among the different locations; ease of coordination of different activities that go on at the different locations.

Marked technological advances in each of these areas over the past two decades have contributed substantially to the economic globalization process.

- Because of advances in transport technology, it has become much easier, faster, and less expensive for a company to move raw materials, intermediate goods, and finished products on a global scale. An icon of how advances in transport technology have advanced the globalization of production and trade is the Boeing 747 cargo jet. Because of its size, speed, and efficiency, the 747 has become a major factor in the international movement of goods. For example, many of the cut flowers sold in the United States are grown in the South American nation of Colombia and placed nightly on 747s to be flown to and sold in the United States. A similar use of 747s has allowed Chilean grapes to grab a major share of the US market. Less dramatic, but just as important, developments in this area include fast transport ships and containerized cargo.

- In the area of communications technology, the advances that have made possible global integration of economic activities are satellite and cellular phone systems and facsimile (fax) machines. These innovations have made it possible for businesses to quickly and efficiently communicate with facilities on a global scale, and thus to be able to locate facilities on a global scale. The telephone system of the emerging economy of Vietnam is being based on these technologies; no phone lines needed!!

- Finally, advances in computer technology, chiefly personal computers, and their linking through local area networks (LANs) and wide area networks, has made it possible for a company headquarters to manage a much larger set of activities spread over a large area than ever before. Thus, a company headquartered in Chicago, or Brussels, or Singapore, can use computer networks to "manage" on a real time basis activities of scores of subsidiary companies or facilities wherever they are located, greatly facilitating global production and marketing operations.

## The Government Factor

However, while the above technological advances are necessary for the global interactions of the world's national economies, they are not sufficient if government policies stand in the way. But, over the past decade, government policies have shifted markedly in favor of business activities and foreign investment.

At the highest level, this shift is exemplified by the decline of communist and socialist economic systems. At the beginning of the 1980s, a large number of planned socialist economies could be enumerated — the USSR, East European countries, Mainland China, Cuba, North Korea, etc. At the end of the 1980s, only Cuba and North Korea remained as rigidly planned socialist economies. In addition, many countries that practiced market socialism also shifted the form of their economic systems more in the direction of capitalism, replacing government with private businesses as the key economic decision making group.

Specific actions these countries' economic reforms took included: selling off state-run economic enterprises (privatization), reducing the number of regulatory hurdles businesses had to surmount to carry out their activities, and removing price controls so businesses could charge what they needed to cover their costs. Moreover, as well as moving toward general pro-business stances, many governments have been making their policies particularly more favorable to investment in their countries by foreign investors.

These countries have:

- allowed foreign investors to be majority owners of their enterprises,

- relaxed constraints on the ability of the foreign businesses to return the profits they earn on their investments to their home company,

- reduced the controls on the movement of investment capital across their borders,

- reduced barriers to the import and export of products the foreign investors used in their economic activities,

- and set foreign exchange rates that were more conducive to attracting foreign investment.

In a recent indication of the extent to which trends such as these are occurring, a United Nations survey of changes in foreign investment laws around the world in 1991 found that of 82 major changes in such laws during that year, 80 had been in the direction of making foreign investment easier.

The shifts have occurred for two reasons. First of all, socialism simply will not produce the efficiencies necessary to maximize the benefits from an economic system. Planned socialism is worst in this regard due to the fact that the central planners simply cannot make the best decisions for a large, complex economy. Even market socialism, however, which eliminates the problems of central planning, falls short due to the fact that it contains too many incentives for inefficiency, such as no one ever gets fired, and too few incentives for efficiency, such as no one is allowed to get rich, at least not through economic activity.

The second reason the shift has occurred has to do with the shift in global production from a slow-moving, natural-resource based process to a fast-moving, technology-based process. In the former situation, while socialism was inefficient, the slow nature of the production process enabled it to mostly keep up. However, as economic production evolved over the 1980s to a technology-driven one, socialism was being left so far behind that it no longer was viable, and, as a result, socialism in its planned form has virtually disappeared, and, in its market form, is disappearing.

## Implications of the New Global Economy

The new global economy has profoundly changed the way national economies work. No longer is a business in a particular country slaved to that country's market for sales nor to its resources for production. With the changes outlined earlier in this chapter, businesses can and do think globally for sales and production decisions.

This new way of thinking has a number of important implications for key groups in countries' economics.

- Businesses that are skilled enough and quick enough can magnify their profits substantially. On the one hand, the new global economy provides them enlarged markets. On the other other hand, the new global economy provides them the ability to produce anywhere in the world. The first result allows them to expand sales, the second to lower costs. US businesses are participating fully in these opportunities, for example, by US telecommunications firms expanding sales in East Asia, and by numerous US firms locating their production facilities in lower-wage countries.

- Because the expansion of the world economy that accompanies these changes raises incomes and demand for better products, the new world economy benefits the skilled labor that is needed to produce these leading edge products. Again, the skilled labor of the United States — in terms of both quantity and quality the best in the world — also benefits.

- All labor in the so-called Third World, or developing countries, benefit as a result of the increased demand for their services from both their own companies who are taking advantage of the greater ease of trade to export products to the industrialized countries and as a result of the massive investment by industrialized countries' companies in the Third World to take advantage of the lower wage rates, less stringent work rules, and ample supplies of labor willing to do low to medium skilled activities. Malaysian real wages, for example, have increased 20 percent over the past five years.

- In contrast, low and medium skilled labor in industrialized countries are not benefiting from the new world economy. This group is losing wages and jobs as a result of the migration of the production of products they work on — textiles, footwear, consumer electronics, etc. — to the lower-cost labor market situations in the Third World. Over the past 20 years of this growing globalization of the world economy, the real wages — actual wages adjusted for inflation — of US production line workers has fallen by 20 percent, compared with an increase of 20 percent in the previous two decades. While in the long run, increased incomes in the Third World may benefit these individuals through increased purchases of US and European products, that benefit does not seem yet about to take hold.

## The Asian Financial Crises and Rethinking the Global Economy

The Asian financial crisis of 1997-98 is causing a rethinking of the impacts of the global economy. In these countries, most of the economic success factors identified in Chapter 11 were present, and yet nearly all have fallen into severe recession. While the meaning of these crises is not fully clear, two strands of thoughts are emerging.

- First, the large flows of portfolio capital into and out of countries may not be as beneficial as thought, and may be harmful. When they flow in, the main impact may be to create an "asset bubble" (overvalued stock and real estate markets), and when they flow out, the main impact is clearly to create currency collapses.

- Second, given the existence of the flows, it is essential for countries to have strong, supervised, open, non-government-influenced financial institutions to ensure that the flows of these funds are well-managed and directed and not wasted.

## Summary

1. Two great, fundamental, changes are altering the way today's economic systems work and impacting on country economies and groups within those economies.

2. The first change is a shift in world production processes from utilizing natural resources and low skilled labor to utilizing technology and high-skilled labor.

3. This change has advantaged countries, groups, and individuals who have the skills to work with technology and disadvantaged countries, groups, and individuals who rely on working with natural resources for their well being.

4. Countries who have taken greatest advantage of this shift includes the United States because of its abundance of technology-creating and using resources, such as educated, disciplined labor and high savings rates.

5. Individuals who have benefited most from this shift are those who are highly educated and trained.

6. Concurrent to the shift in the bases for economic activity, the national economic systems of the world, including that of the United States, are becoming ever more linked with economic trends in other countries and the world economy.

7. These growing linkages are linking national economies across a wide range of economic activities — trade, investment, ownership and technology — and are magnifying the impact of the first shift.

8. Growth in these linkages is being driven by advances in technology — especially in transportation, communication, and computers — and changes in government policies to more favorable to business activity and foreign investment and trade.

9. Businesses, including US, by and large are benefiting from these changes, from being able to access more markets, being able to access low-cost production locations, and having access to the strong technology resources of the US economy.

10. Skilled labor, especially US, benefits as a result of the positive impact on demand for their skills of the advances in the world economy related to the globalization process.

11. Low and medium skilled labor in the developing countries benefit as low and medium technology production processes are shifted there to take advantage of their lower wages.

12. In contrast, low and medium skilled labor in the industrialized countries, including the United States, are disadvantaged as much of what they used to do comes to be done in lower-wage, less-advanced countries.

# Index to Key Terms and Concepts